Will the Real Paul Revere Please Stand Up?

And 14 Other American History Plays

by Gail Skroback Hennessey

SCHOLASTIC
PROFESSIONAL**B**OOKS

New York ✳ Toronto ✳ London ✳ Auckland ✳ Sydney

Mexico City ✳ New Delhi ✳ Hong Kong ✳ Buenos Aires

⋆ Dedication ⋆

To Dad, Mom, and Cliff . . . always in my heart.
Thank you for your encouragement and support
in the pursuit of my dreams!

⋆ Acknowledgment ⋆

Special thanks go to Mark Goodson Productions for granting
permission to adapt this concept for use in these plays.

Cover design by Jim Sarfati
Cover illustration by Mike Moran
Interior design by Kelli Thompson
Interior illustrations by Mike Moran

ISBN: 0-439-09842-4

Printed in the U.S.A.

Contents

Introduction

Do your students love game shows? Then they'll have a blast with these fact-filled plays about famous people in America's past! What a great way for young people to learn about 15 historic figures that contributed so much to the world in which we live.

The format of these plays is based on a game show that originated in the mid-1950s called *To Tell the Truth*. On that show, four celebrities appeared before a panel of guests, each claiming to be someone of note, such as the inventor of Silly Putty®, or the record-holder for the world's largest bubble gum bubble. Only the real guest had to respond truthfully; the impostors could answer however they pleased. The goal of the guests was to try to stump the celebrities.

Why I Wrote the Book

One of the reasons I developed these plays is that I wanted to show students that famous people were youngsters once, just like they are. They dealt with issues similar to those that your own students face. What did Ben Franklin do when he had problems with his math homework? Did Nellie Bly get along with her brothers? What kind of relationship did Abraham Lincoln and his stepmother have? My hope is that, by reading these plays, students will not only learn more about these historic figures, but also get a sense of their humanity. Each one started life like everyone else—as a typical young person. Students should also note that, in each case, fame came as a result of hard work, perseverance, and commitment to a goal—things that anyone dedicated to a dream can achieve. I hope you will find the plays to be as valuable a learning tool in your classroom as I have.

How the Book Is Arranged

Each play is followed by a Teacher's Page which includes discussion questions, activity ideas, and a brief review of the historical accuracy of some key comments made by the panelists. For example, in the play about Paul Revere, one of the Reveres states that, as a silversmith, he once was hired to make a silver collar for someone's pet squirrel. Believe it or not, this tid-bit is true!

You'll also find many ways that you can incorporate these plays into your social studies, reading, language arts, or science curriculum. The Additional Resources section includes literature and Internet links for each famous American featured in this book.

Finally, the game show format also demands that students use critical thinking to distinguish the "impostors" from the "real" guest. Be sure to encourage students with speaking parts to really try and hone their acting skills, staying aware of intonation, and how well their voices carry. Also, keep in mind that they're great as Friday change-of-pace activities, or as a treat just before a holiday break. I'm sure you'll find many more ways to make the best use of these plays for the way that you teach.

How to Use the Plays in Your Classroom

The 15 biographical plays are all student-directed. I usually choose a "Host," and then allow that youngster to select fellow classmates for the remaining speaking parts. These students—the host, biographer, panelists, and guests—all take seats in front of the classroom. The "viewers"—those without speaking roles—are also given a copy of the play, too, so everyone can read along as the subject's history unfolds.

As an alternative, you as the teacher may want to play the Host. Though a very small speaking part, the Host explains the rules of the game and moderates the panel. This option may make sense in classrooms with discipline problems, or in those where extra guidance is required.

Reading the Play

Before distributing each play, hold a brief discussion to find out what students already know about the famous American. Then, as the play is being performed, consider pausing between one or more of the panelists' questions to review the information that students hear. Invite opinions about which actor is most likely the "real" historical figure, encouraging students to share their reasoning. Remind the class that only the real one must always tell the truth.

Will the Real Christopher Columbus Please Stand Up?

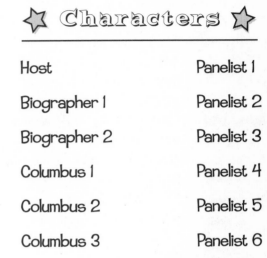

☆ Characters ☆

Host	Panelist 1
Biographer 1	Panelist 2
Biographer 2	Panelist 3
Columbus 1	Panelist 4
Columbus 2	Panelist 5
Columbus 3	Panelist 6
	Panelist 7

Host: Welcome to *To Tell the Truth*! Today's guest is Christopher Columbus, the Genoese explorer who sailed across the Atlantic Ocean looking for a trade route to the Indies. Instead, he came across lands that the people of Europe had never even seen before. Only one of our three guests is the real Christopher Columbus. The other two are impostors. Listen carefully to what each one says. Then it's up to you to figure out who's telling the truth, the whole truth, and nothing but the truth. Let's begin by meeting our guests.

Columbus 1: Ahoy, students. My name is Christopher Columbus.

Columbus 2: It is an honor to be your guest today. My name is Christopher Columbus.

Columbus 3: Hello, everybody. I'm Christopher Columbus.

Biographer 1: Before we start, the real Christopher Columbus has asked us to read this letter of introduction to you:

Dear Students: I, Christopher Columbus, was born around 1451, when the Age of Discovery was just beginning. Many Europeans at that time were hoping to find a new route to India—especially because the Turks had closed off the only land routes there. That made it hard for Europeans like myself to reach the gold, silver, and precious spices of the Indies. My goal was to find a shorter route by going west, something no European before me had ever tried to do.

Biographer 2: *(continues reading the letter)*

> Eventually I made four trips across what we used to call the Ocean Sea. Today you call it the Atlantic Ocean. I truly believed that I had reached China. Little did I know that instead I had stumbled across a land mass previously unknown to Europeans. I died in 1506, never really knowing the impact that I had made on the world. Signed, Christopher Columbus.

Host: Let's begin the questioning with Panelist 1.

Panelist 1: As a child, your only formal education came from the weavers' guild that your family belonged to. You learned a bit of math, writing, and reading from them. So what first sparked your interest in sailing?

Columbus 1: It was Marco Polo's book on his adventures in China. In it he described all the riches that he found there. That book convinced me to become an explorer. I read it over and over again!

Columbus 2: At about fourteen, I started to go with my father on his sea voyages to sell cloth. It was on those trips that I learned how to steer a ship, handle the rigging, and hoist an anchor. I loved the sea! Dad didn't, though. He always tried to stay within sight of the shore!

Columbus 3: Genoa, Italy, where I grew up, was an important sea-trading route for European merchants. The stories that I heard there really had an effect on me. They got me interested in sailing.

Panelist 2: At the age of twenty-five something terrible happened. You were sailing off the coast of Portugal when your ship was attacked by French pirates. The ship went down in flames and you alone survived. You grabbed a floating oar and clung to it for six miles, kicking your way to shore. How did your life change after this experience?

Columbus 1: Ugh! That was horrible. But good things happened to me once I reached Portugal. After all, it was the place to learn how to sail back then. Before his death, Prince Henry the Navigator had opened the first school for mariners there. Eventually I ran a bookstore in Lisbon that also sold maps. Sailors would come in and I'd hear them describe their incredible adventures in faraway lands.

Columbus 2: After surviving that incident, I came to believe that God had saved my life for a reason. After all, I was named after Saint Christopher, the patron saint of travelers. I decided that my purpose in life must be to spread Christianity across the Ocean Sea.

Columbus 3: After settling in Portugal, I met my first wife, Felipa. It turned out that her family had friends in the court of Portugal's King John. This gave me the "in" I needed to meet the King so I could ask him to fund my westward voyage to the Indies.

Columbus 1: Yes. Many members of my crew were frightened. We all knew that Earth was round. But we didn't know how big it was. I was even afraid to tell my crew how far we traveled on that first journey. So I made up a phony ship's log that showed us going fewer miles each day than I thought we really had. If my crew had known I was doing that, forget it! There would have been a mutiny for sure!

Columbus 2: Afraid? No way! My crew and I were not wimps! We may have worried a bit about being in the sun all day. But even that wasn't a problem. We just made sure to pack plenty of sunscreen.

Columbus 3: It never even crossed our minds to worry about the voyage. We were too busy thinking about the riches we would find!

Panelist 4: On August 3, 1492, the Niña, the Pinta, and the Santa Maria finally set sail with about one hundred men and enough food to last a year. When you and your crew reached the thick seaweed of the Sargasso Sea, your ships could barely move through it. Later your crew saw a meteor streak across the sky and took it as a bad omen of things to come. What else do you remember about that voyage?

Columbus 1: More than once I heard rumors that some of my men were thinking of tossing me overboard. Luckily for me, we spotted land before they ever tried this!

Columbus 2: To help us pass the long days out at sea, we did a lot of fishing. This kept us busy and supplied us with many of our meals.

Columbus 3: There wasn't much to do aboard the ships. So, to pass the time, I'd play my kazoo and we'd have dance contests. Of course, being the captain, I always won!

Panelist 5: On October 12, 1492, you arrived in what you thought were the Indies. That's why you dubbed the natives "Indians." Really, though, you had landed near Cuba. The people you met there were kind and gentle. They offered you and your men food and gifts. Still, you were disappointed by how little gold you saw. What other memories do you have of the natives that you met on that first trip?

Columbus 1: The natives were helpful. When the Santa Maria hit a coral reef, hundreds of them came to help us unload the ship before it sank. I was very grateful.

Columbus 2: The natives joined my crew for a big feast to celebrate our arrival. We had turkey, cranberries, mashed potatoes, and pumpkin pie. Yum! It was a great dinner for giving thanks.

Columbus 3:   The natives were very excited by all the goodies I had brought with me from Europe. They had never seen horses, cattle, or donkeys before! In exchange for these, they gave us lots of corn, tobacco, and potatoes—all of which were new to us.

Panelist 6:   On each return trip, you treated the natives worse and worse. When you couldn't find any of the legendary gold-digging ants you had read about, you forced them to work in mines digging gold for you instead. If they didn't bring back enough, they were punished. Many died and others ran away. Then, adding insult to injury, you decided to take some natives back to Europe with you as slaves. Do you have anything to say in your defense, Mr. Columbus?

Columbus 1:   Since the native people were not Christians like me, I didn't see anything wrong with taking them to be sold as slaves. Besides, the explorers of Africa were also doing this, and I needed some profit to please the queen.

Columbus 2:   I never did anything but show kindness to the natives. It was my crew—not me—that was mean to these people.

Columbus 3:   The natives begged me to bring them back with us to Europe. They were all incredibly curious to see how we lived.

Panelist 7:   By your fourth and final trip across the Atlantic, you had traveled much of the Caribbean. You even came close to the Pacific Ocean when you reached present-day Panama. Yet, you continued to think you were in the Indies. What else comes to mind when you think about these adventures?

Columbus 1:   Scientific knowledge I had learned over the years proved very useful in the land you now call Jamaica. We were in need of food, but the leader of Jamaica wouldn't help us. It was February 28, and I remembered an eclipse would be occurring the next day, blackening the day sky.   When it occurred, I angrily told the leader," I have taken away the sun since you refused to feed my men or me!" Fortunately, he changed his mind before the eclipse passed a few hours later.

Columbus 2:   My men and I finally found the gold we were looking for and built a huge golden arch by our fort. Some of the crew came up with the idea of selling hamburgers to the local population, and I posted a sign stating how many we sold each day.

Columbus 3:   Are you sure I didn't get to the Indies? That's terrible! So all my travels were just a waste of time? What a failure I was!

Host: Okay, everyone. It is now time to decide who you think is the real Christopher Columbus. With a show of hands, how many think it is Columbus 1? *(pause)* Columbus 2? *(pause)* Columbus 3? *(pause)* Now that everyone has voted, let's have the real Christopher Columbus please stand up.

Will the Real Christopher Columbus Please Stand Up?
☆ Teacher's Page ☆

Who Is the Real Christopher Columbus?

Once all the votes have been cast, establish that Christopher Columbus 1 is the real Columbus. Then review the play, making sure students can distinguish all of these true and false statements:

Panelists 1 and 2: All responses to the questions are true.

Panelist 3: There was no sunscreen (and most likely no fear of being in the sun all day) in Columbus' time. But many of the crew were worried about crossing the Atlantic. In fact, Columbus had a hard time recruiting sailors because so many feared the voyage.

Panelist 4: When the waters were calm, Columbus' crew did fish and then cook their catch. It is unlikely, however, that they danced or played the kazoo! To pass the time, the sailors would pray, sing songs, tell stories, do chores, eat, and star-gaze.

Panelist 5: There are no records of a feast between Columbus' crew and the Native Americans. Columbus 2 is referring to Thanksgiving, which first took place in Plymouth, Massachusetts, over one hundred years after Columbus died. And, though the Native Americans did introduce Columbus to products like corn, tobacco, and potatoes, he did not bring horses, cattle, or donkeys along until his second trip.

Panelist 6: Neither Columbus 2 nor 3 is being honest here. Discuss with students how and why the relationship between Columbus and the Native Americans deteriorated over time.

Panelist 7: Though Columbus did find some gold and other riches on his voyages, it was never in the huge quantities that he had expected. As for the comment that Columbus 3 makes, solicit students' opinions as to whether or not Columbus was a failure. Point out, of course, that until his dying day, he truly believed that he had reached the Orient by traveling west.

Questions for Discussion

1. Find Italy on a map of the world. Why do you think it was such an important trading route in Columbus' day?

2. In what ways did the Age of Exploration change the world forever?

3. Overall, do you think Columbus made positive contributions to the world, or negative ones? What makes you think so?

Activities

1. Write a diary entry pretending you were a sailor on the Niña, the Pinta, or the Santa Maria. In your log, describe a typical day at sea.

2. Imagine you are a Native American in 1492, seeing Columbus and his crew for the first time. In a paragraph, describe your reaction.

3. Put Christopher Columbus on trial for the way he treated the Native Americans. Assign a student lawyer to represent each side.

Will the Real Benjamin Franklin Please Stand Up?

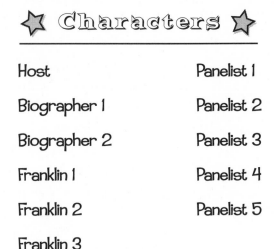

☆ Characters ☆

Host	Panelist 1
Biographer 1	Panelist 2
Biographer 2	Panelist 3
Franklin 1	Panelist 4
Franklin 2	Panelist 5
Franklin 3	

Host: Welcome to *To Tell the Truth*! Today's guest is Benjamin Franklin, American writer, printer, philosopher, scientist, and statesman. Only one of our three guests is the real Benjamin Franklin. The other two are impostors. Listen carefully to what each one says. Then it's up to you to figure out who's telling the truth, the whole truth, and nothing but the truth. Let's begin by meeting our guests.

Franklin 1: Hello. My name is Benjamin Franklin.

Franklin 2: Greetings, students. I am Benjamin Franklin.

Franklin 3: Hi. I'm Ben Franklin. And if you don't believe me, you can go fly a kite!

Biographer 1: Before we start, the real Benjamin Franklin has asked us to read this letter of introduction to you:

Dear Students: I, Benjamin Franklin, was born in Boston, Massachusetts, in 1706, seventy years before the thirteen colonies declared their independence from England. I am the only person to have signed all four major documents that helped define the new nation—the Declaration of Independence, the Treaty of Alliance with France, the Treaty of Peace with Great Britain, and the Constitution of the United States. Thomas Jefferson once called me "the greatest man and ornament of the age and country in which he lived."

Biographer 2: *(continues reading the letter)*

> People also remember me as an inventor and writer. In my day, I sold over ten thousand copies a year of my *Poor Richard's Almanack*. In it you could find recipes and sayings, plus facts about weather and farming. I used to argue that the turkey should be declared our national bird. Of course, I was out-voted on that one. All my life I lived by this simple motto: "Improve yourself." I died in 1790, at the age of eighty-four. Signed, Benjamin Franklin.

Host: Let's begin the questioning with Panelist 1.

Panelist 1: Like other craftsmen of the time, Mr. Franklin, your father was known as a "leather apron man," because of what he wore when he made his soap and candles. I'm sure he worked very hard to support the seventeen children in your family. How did you spend your time before you were old enough to learn a trade?

Franklin 1: Well, I loved to swim and would play for hours in the water. One windy day, as an experiment, I had a kite pull me across a mile-wide pond. A friend came and carried my clothes for me. Otherwise, I would have had to run back around the pond naked! In those days, our birthday suits were the only bathing suits we owned!

Franklin 2: With seventeen kids in my family, I didn't often get extra spending money. But one day when I did have some, I happened to see a young boy with a whistle. I wanted that whistle so badly, I gave him all my money for it. When I got home, my parents told me that I could have bought four times as much at a general store. Later when I saw people overpaying for things, I'd exclaim, "They give too much for their whistles!"

Franklin 3: Not everyone back in my day had the chance to go to school. But my parents sent me because they hoped I would become a preacher. I could read even before I started going. But I was terrible at math. Two years later, when I was ten, I dropped out to help my father in his business. I did continue to read a lot, though. I even improved my math skills by reading books on math!

Panelist 2: As a teenager, you became an apprentice in your older brother's printing business. But you and he never got along very well. Even though you were under contract to work there until you were twenty-one, you ran away at age seventeen. In fact, you walked fifty miles in the rain from New Jersey to Pennsylvania with very little money. Describe what it was like working with your brother before you left home.

Franklin 1: I always found James to be too bossy. Since he wouldn't let me write for his newspaper, I submitted articles to it under the phony name "Silence Dogood." Even my brother loved this mysterious writer's work. But when he learned it was me—boy, was he angry!

Franklin 2: I had one good deal with my brother. Rather than feed me, he agreed to pay me half of what my meals would cost him. With the cash, I put myself on a healthy vegetarian diet of bread, raisins, and water. Then, with the money I saved, I treated myself to books.

Franklin 3: At that time, many people were dying from a disease called smallpox. Vaccinations against such diseases were not common then, as they are now. But a man named Increase Mather had an idea for a vaccine against smallpox. I never understood why my brother wrote against that idea. To me it made a lot of sense.

Panelist 3: Soon after arriving in Philadelphia, you found work as a printer. But while living there, you did so much more! You helped found an insurance company, a hospital, a fire department, and the first public library in America. You also invented the Franklin stove, bifocal glasses, and a glass harmonica, among other things. After tripping in a mud puddle late one night, you suggested the idea of street lamps. And we can't forget your famous experiment involving a silk kite, a key, and an electrical storm. Tell us more about your scientific work, Mr. Franklin.

Franklin 1: This may shock you, but people were so interested in my experiments with electricity that they would actually pay to get a shock from me. I once invited a number of people to an "electric picnic" where I planned to roast a turkey on electric circuits. Unfortunately, I accidentally knocked myself unconscious first!

Franklin 2: I once did some experiments about the intelligence of ants. That's right—ants! I filled a pot with molasses and hung it on a string. Then I watched as an ant crawled along the string to get to the pot. Soon there were many ants crawling up that string, proving to me that ants must have a way of communicating with each other.

Franklin 3: Like many people, I hated getting out of bed once I was under the covers. So I came up with a way to bolt my door without getting up. All I had to do was pull a cord strung from my bed to the door. That moved a latch, which locked the door. It worked great!

Panelist 4: Your witty sayings include "A penny saved is a penny earned," and "Well done is better than well said." Can you share any of your other expressions with us?

Franklin 1: I wrote the line, "I came, I saw, I conquered," for Julius Caesar of Rome. But later he took all the credit for it.

Franklin 2: I once said, "Fish and visitors smell in three days." You can be sure I tried never to outstay my welcome!

Franklin 3: Have you ever heard the song "Zippity Doo-Da"? That catchy saying of mine was later put to music and sung by a dancing cricket named Jiminy.

Panelist 5:   In your later life, your achievements were recognized on both sides of the Atlantic. When you visited royalty in Europe, you would always dress simply and wear your coonskin hat. You were called America's best arguer. But as good a statesmen as you were, you could not reach a peaceful settlement with the British that would have prevented the American Revolution. You did, however, successfully gain support for the colonists' cause from other European nations, especially France. Any final comments, sir?

Franklin 1:   I don't mean to brag, but my coonskin hat started a huge fashion craze in Europe. To this day, these caps have stayed in vogue.

Franklin 2:   Well, I don't mean to brag either, but when I finally returned from Europe, I was honored with parades and cannon salutes. Bells rang all over town. Even though I was seventy-nine years old, the people elected me three years in a row as president of the Pennsylvania government!

Franklin 3:   You guys can brag all you want. But when I was in France, I became the one millionth visitor to EuroDisney. I got a lifetime pass to the amusement park and a huge stuffed Mickey Mouse for my granddaughter!

Host: Okay, everyone. It is now time to decide who you think is the real Benjamin Franklin. With a show of hands, how many think it is Franklin 1? *(pause)* Franklin 2? *(pause)* Franklin 3? *(pause)* Now that everyone has voted, let's have the real Benjamin Franklin please stand up.

Will the Real Benjamin Franklin Please Stand Up?
✪ Teacher's Page ✪

Who Is the Real Benjamin Franklin?

Once all the votes have been cast, establish that Benjamin Franklin 2 is the real Franklin. Then review the play, making sure students can distinguish all of these true and false statements:

Panelists 1, 2 and 3: All responses to the questions are true.

Panelist 4: Julius Caesar (100–44 B.C.) lived over a thousand years before Franklin did, so obviously Franklin 1 is lying. Likewise, Ben Franklin was not known for nonsensical phrases like "Zippity Doo-Da." Thus, Franklin 3 is lying as well.

Panelist 5: Although Franklin's unusual styles did start a fashion craze in Europe at the height of his popularity, it has long since died down. As for EuroDisney, it did not open until 1992, over two hundred years after Franklin's death.

Questions for Discussion

1. What do you think it would have been like to grow up as one of 17 children, the way Ben Franklin did? How do you think this might have affected him?

2. If you had been Ben Franklin, what might you have said to King George III to try to prevent the American Revolution?

3. If Ben Franklin could see the way the world looks now, what kind of reaction to it do you think he would have?

Activities

1. Write a rap song or a poem about one of Ben Franklin's inventions.

2. As a class, create a time line of Ben Franklin's accomplishments. See how big the timeline can become!

3. Challenge each student to create a poster that illustrates the meaning of a saying from *Poor Richard's Almanack*.

Will the Real Daniel Boone Please Stand Up?

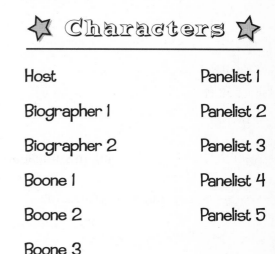

☆ **Characters** ☆

Host	Panelist 1
Biographer 1	Panelist 2
Biographer 2	Panelist 3
Boone 1	Panelist 4
Boone 2	Panelist 5
Boone 3	

Host: Welcome to *To Tell the Truth*! Today's guest is Daniel Boone, one of this nation's greatest frontiersmen. Only one of our three guests is the real Daniel Boone. The other two are impostors. Listen carefully to what each one says. Then it's up to you to figure out who's telling the truth, the whole truth, and nothing but the truth. Let's begin by meeting our guests.

Boone 1: Hello. I am Daniel Boone, wilderness pioneer. Thanks for letting me join you today.

Boone 2: What an adventure! I've never been inside a school before. My name is Daniel Boone.

Boone 3: Greetings, students. My name is Daniel Boone. Now has anyone seen my coonskin hat? I can't remember where I left it!

Biographer 1: Before we start, the real Daniel Boone asked us to read this letter of introduction to you:

Dear Students: I, Daniel Boone, was born in 1734 to a Quaker family in what is now the state of Pennsylvania. When I was sixteen, my father decided that the area had become too crowded, so we moved to North Carolina. Four years later, I barely escaped with my life as I fought with the British at the battle of Fort Duquesne during the French and Indian War. While there, a man named John Finley described to me a beautiful place called "Kentucky," on the other side of the Appalachian Mountains. After that, I went back home where I married Rebecca Bryan. But later, in 1767, I joined Finley and four others to explore this land for myself.

Biographer 2: *(continues reading the letter)*

> Once I saw Kentucky, I was hooked. I kept going back. At that time, only Native Americans lived west of the Appalachians, and it wasn't easy to find a safe route through that huge mountain range. I was even captured by Shawnee a few times. But I always escaped. Later, a man named Richard Henderson hired me to help blaze a Wilderness Road through a section of the mountain known as "Cumberland Gap." Westward expansion really grew after that. Eventually my wife and daughter became the first white women to see Kentucky. I died at the ripe old age of eighty-six. Signed, Daniel Boone.

Host: Let's begin the questioning with Panelist 1.

Panelist 1: As a child, one of your aunts taught you to read and write. Your parents taught you weaving and the blacksmith trade. But you never received any formal education. "Let the girls learn to spell," your father would say, "and Dan will do the shooting." What else do you remember about your childhood?

Boone 1: I loved to roam around outdoors. But when I was about six, there was a smallpox outbreak. My mom was so worried, she decided to keep us kids inside. Of course, I hated that. So I snuck over to the house of a boy who had smallpox and climbed into bed with him. I guess I just wanted to get the disease over with. I did get it, too. So did my brothers and sisters. But luckily, we all got better.

Boone 2: Before I was old enough to have a gun, I made a sharp javelin from a tree branch and used it to hunt with. By my twelfth birthday, I had become an expert hunter and trapper. That day, my father gave me my first long-barreled flintlock rifle. I named it "Tick Licker," and took it with me everywhere I went.

Boone 3: When I was young, I was put in charge of caring for my family's cattle. Watching those cows could get pretty boring. So, to pass the time, I started singing at the top of my lungs. Once, a Shawnee boy came along and started singing with me. He and I became friends. He showed me how to use a bow and arrow, and even invited me to his tribe where I ate, using a leaf for a plate. My mother disapproved of my friendships with Indians.

Panelist 2: Though you learned a lot from Native Americans as a youth, you later ran into problems with them. You were one of many that they tried to convince to move back east by using force. Once you were cornered on three sides, and found that the only way to escape was to jump off of a cliff! You fell about sixty feet, then landed in a tree and waved up at your attackers. What other encounters did you have with Native Americans?

Boone 1:   Once I was captured with two other men. The Shawnee took our horses and rifles, plus hundreds of buckskins and beaver pelts that we had collected. Then they let us go. We were furious! So we followed them back to their camp and retook the horses. Unfortunately, the Shawnees recaptured us and this time they made us prisoners. They placed a bell around my neck and forced me to dance, which was not a pretty sight, I admit. Eventually we escaped.

Boone 2:   During the Revolutionary War, the British armed some Native American groups and encouraged them to attack our settlements. One group captured my daughter and two other girls. But my Jemima had learned a trick or two from her old dad. Pretending that their feet hurt, the girls cut their dresses to use as bandages. Then they left a trail of cloth so we could find them. Also, they kept falling off their horses on purpose to stall the Indians. Eventually we rescued them, but in the process I was almost killed before a buddy rescued me!

Boone 3:   I could sit here all day and tell you Indian stories! Once I was captured at a salt spring near Boonesboro, Kentucky. Yes, that settlement was named after me. Anyway, the chief of the Shawnee adopted me and named me "Big Turtle." But when I heard that they planned to attack Boonesboro, I escaped and ran for four days—about one hundred sixty miles—to warn everyone. We wound up fighting those Shawnee for nine days, but eventually we got them to leave.

Panelist 3:   It's no wonder that, to this day, "buck" and "dough" are popular slang terms for money. Both date back to frontier times when people like you sold buck skins and doe hides for cash. You'd sometimes stay in the woods for weeks at a time on one of your "long hunts." And, though you said that you never got lost in the woods, you did admit to being bewildered once for three days. Sometimes, word has it, you'd carve things into the trees as you wandered the frontier. Tell us: What kinds of things did you carve?

Boone 1:   Awe, shucks. I can't tell a lie. I liked to carve hearts in the trees. Then I'd write my initials next to those of my wife.

Boone 2:   Sometimes I wrote my name and the date that I passed through an area on a tree. Could I get into trouble for that?

Boone 3:   As a joke, I'd sometimes carve the words "Peek a boo!" on a tree. Then I'd hide and wait 'til someone I knew came along. When they did, I'd jump out at them and yell "surprise!"

Panelist 4:   Richard Henderson, who hired you to build the Wilderness Road, convinced the Cherokees to sell him Kentucky for trinkets. He gave many acres of this land to you. But some tribes, like the Shawnee, didn't honor the sale. That led to trouble. Two of your children even died at the hands of Native Americans who were angry at people like you who wanted the land. Were you ever involved in any other land disputes?

Boone 1: No. Actually, Henderson's generosity soon made me rich. So my wife and I built a mansion, and I never worked another day in my life. You can still visit our old Kentucky home today.

Boone 2: Well, I was. And it still hurts to talk about it. First I had all that land. Then wham-o! It was gone. As it turned out, none of the land deeds I had were considered legal—even though I'd settled so much of the area myself! This made me so mad that I moved my family to Missouri in 1799. There the Spanish honored me, calling me a trailblazer. They rewarded me with about 840 acres of my own. But the United States bought that land from France in the Louisiana Purchase, and I was out of luck again! For a time, I was actually completely broke!

Boone 3: There were no land disputes for me. I loved Kentucky so much that I wrote a popular tune called "My Old Kentucky Home." Imagine how proud I was to hear in my old age that it had been made the official state song!

Panelist 5: In 1781, you were elected to the Virginia legislature. (Kentucky was considered a part of Virginia then.) Yet you really preferred adventure. In your late seventies, you even wanted to fight in the War of 1812, but were told that you were too old. Still, even at that age, you kept exploring. What else did you do in your later life?

Boone 1: When I finally retired, I took up horse racing. I started an event called the "Kentucky Felt Hat," after a famous cap I always wore. But a friend told me that derbies were more popular. So I renamed my race the "Kentucky Derby." Maybe you've heard of it?

Boone 2: In 1810, the United States Congress finally voted to restore my land titles in honor of my many years of service to the country. But they never gave me nearly as much land as I'd settled. I even had to sell some of what they did give me to pay off my debts!

Boone 3: After my wife Rebecca died, I retired to Florida. It was somewhere that I'd considered moving when I was younger, but I could never convince Rebecca that she'd like it there. It was nice to live where it was always warm and peaceful in my later years.

Host: Okay, everyone. It is now time to decide who you think is the real Daniel Boone. With a show of hands, how many think it is Boone 1? *(pause)* Boone 2? *(pause)* Boone 3? *(pause)* Now that everyone has voted, let's have the real Daniel Boone please stand up.

DANIEL BOONE (1734-1820)

Will the Real Daniel Boone Please Stand Up?
☆ Teacher's Page ☆

Who Is the Real Daniel Boone?

Once all the votes have been cast, establish that Daniel Boone 2 is the real Boone. Then review the play, making sure that students can distinguish all of these true and false statements:

Panelist 1 and 2: All responses to the questions are true.

Panelist 3: Though all three responses sound silly, only Boone 2 is telling the truth.

Panelist 4: As the panelist's question implies, land was always a big issue for Daniel Boone. He never got rich and he was constantly involved in land disputes, as Boone 2 says. As for the song, "My Old Kentucky Home," it was written by Stephen Foster in 1853 and wasn't adopted as Kentucky's state song until 1928.

Panelist 5: The first Kentucky Derby wasn't held until 1875, 50 years after Boone's death. And, though Boone did visit Florida and think about moving there earlier in his life, he never actually did.

Questions for Discussion

1. What did you know about Daniel Boone before you read this play? Does anything that you learned about him here surprise you?

2. Based on what you now know, what values does it seem Boone was taught as a child? How do these compare with the values that you are learning in school and at home?

3. How might Daniel Boone's life have been different if he had lived in an age with TVs and computers? How would your life be different if you had lived in an age without them?

4. How did Daniel Boone's relationship with the Native Americans seem to change as he got older? Why do you think this change took place?

Activities

1. Although Daniel Boone was a real person, he was also the stuff of legends. Research some ways that his life stories have been used in fictional accounts of the "wild west." Then write your own made-up wild west adventure, and include Boone as a character in your story.

2. Fold a sheet of paper in half. On one side, draw a log cabin. On the other, draw your home. Next to the cabin, write five reasons why it would have been favorable to live in Daniel Boone's time. Next to the picture of your home, write five favorable things about life now.

Will the Real Paul Revere Please Stand Up?

☆ Characters ☆

Host	Panelist 1
Biographer 1	Panelist 2
Biographer 2	Panelist 3
Revere 1	Panelist 4
Revere 2	Panelist 5
Revere 3	

Host: Hi! Welcome to *To Tell the Truth*! Today's guest is Paul Revere, the famous silversmith, engraver, and Revolutionary War hero. Only one of our three guests is the real Paul Revere. The other two are impostors. Listen carefully to what each one says. Then it's up to you to figure out who's telling the truth, the whole truth, and nothing but the truth. Let's begin by meeting our guests.

Revere 1: Let's not "horse around." There's too much I want to tell you about myself! My name is Paul Revere.

Revere 2: Good day to all you students. My name is Paul Revere.

Revere 3: That can't be—because my name is Paul Revere!

Biographer 1: Before we start, the real Paul Revere has asked us to read this letter of introduction to you:

Dear Students: I, Paul Revere, was born in Boston, Massachusetts, on New Year's Day, 1735. I was a skilled silversmith and a Patriot devoted to helping the colonies free themselves from British rule. Disguised as a Native American, I was one of many who threw tea into the harbor during the Boston Tea Party. I was also often asked to carry messages among the colonies on horseback.

Biographer 2: *(continues reading the letter)*

You've probably heard about my most famous ride. Right before the first battles of the Revolutionary War at Lexington and Concord, I helped warn the colonists of the approaching British. Years later, Henry Wadsworth Longfellow wrote a well-known poem about it called "Paul Revere's Ride." I also made gunpowder, cannons, and even printed money for the Massachusetts colony. And I was famous for the bells that I made. Of the 398 bells that I crafted in my lifetime, 75 still hang within the church steeples of New England. I died in 1818, at the age of eighty-three. Signed, Paul Revere.

Host: Let's begin the questioning with Panelist 1.

Panelist 1: Like many young men in your day, Mr. Revere, you went to school until you were thirteen. Then you left to learn how to be a silversmith from your dad. Please tell us more about your childhood.

Revere 1: In school I learned reading, writing, and mathematics. Those who did poorly were sent to a corner wearing a dunce cap. But not me! Like the other good students, sometimes I was even rewarded with cakes. My teacher was really sorry when I left school. But I promised to always do my best in whatever I did in life.

Revere 2: I was proud to be one of seven boys who rang the bells at Boston's Christ Church. We rang them on Sundays and holidays, and whenever there was a fire, important meeting, or any big news. Each of us had a rope to pull. The trick was to pull them the right way, so they would echo beautifully throughout the town.

Revere 3: Even as a child I must have dreamed of an independent United States. One day, while ringing the bells, a friend said that his father liked to think the bells rang for God and England. But I thought they rang for America. It's funny how years later, it was from the very same steeple that I had a message sent, alerting other colonists of the British soldiers' plans.

Panelist 2: Before the American Revolution, you fought with the British at Lake George, New York, during the French and Indian War. Tell us a bit about that.

Revere 1: Actually, there's not very much to tell. I was twenty-one and I was away from home for the first time. My biggest battle was keeping those horrible black flies away from me! As a soldier, I had hoped for a little bit more excitement than that.

Revere 2:   You would never have known that the British were fighting on the same side as us—not the way they treated us, anyway. They teased us for not having uniforms. And they called us "funny doodles," or "Yankee Doodles of Massachusetts." Once, out of frustration, I told someone that "I'd rather fight the English than the French!" Later, that's exactly what I wound up doing!

Revere 3:   I agree. We weren't even allowed to have a higher rank than a British officer. I once asked a fellow colonist why, if we were all English, we weren't treated the same. But he said that we were Americans, not English. That idea stayed with me. Then, after the French and Indian War, King George III raised our taxes to pay off his war debt. Believe me, I wasn't the only one to get angry!

Panelist 3:   As a silversmith you made shoe and belt buckles, baby rattles, tea pots, and things like that. What else did you do?

Revere 1:   With eleven mouths to feed, I was always on the lookout for extra ways to make money—especially with silver so expensive back then! I even tried my hand at dentistry. In my day, there were no such things as fillings. Decayed teeth were just pulled out. Then people needed artificial teeth, like the ones I made from sheep teeth and hippopotamus tusks, so they could speak clearly and eat.

Revere 2:   Once a rich man in town had an odd request for me. He hired me to make him a silver collar for his pet squirrel!

Revere 3:   Every parent during that time wanted their child to be born with a silver spoon in its mouth. So I kept busy for many years cranking out silver spoons! But at least it paid the rent!

Panelist 4:   In modern times, some historians have criticized the engraving you made of the event that came to be called the "Boston Massacre." After all, it wasn't a very accurate picture of what happened, was it? Why was that? And what else did you do in pre Revolutionary Boston to further the patriot cause?

Revere 1:   Of course, I can't say for sure what happened at the Boston Massacre. I wasn't there. The British were probably just defending themselves. After all, colonists threw things at them all the time. Still, they had no right to shoot anybody! I wanted my engraving to make people angry at the British—and that's exactly what it did!

Revere 2:   As I said in my letter of introduction, on December 16, 1773, I helped dump three hundred forty-two chests of British tea into Boston Harbor. There were about ten thousand pounds of the stuff! But the biggest role I played in that event came afterward when I rode sixty-three miles a day for eleven days, telling other colonists what we had done.

Revere 3: Actually, my biggest contribution to the Boston Tea Party was discovering that if you scoop tea leaves up in a handkerchief and then dunk the hankie in hot water, you don't wind up with loose tea leaves in your mouth when you drink. Today, you take tea bags for granted. But I invented the very first one.

Panelist 5: Earlier, you mentioned your famous ride of 1775. You and William Dawes were sent to warn Samuel Adams and John Hancock that the British commander, General Gage, had ordered soldiers to the city of Concord. Their mission was to destroy weapons that the patriots had stored there. Tell us more about that night, Mr. Revere.

Revere 1: Can you believe that when I left for my ride, I forgot my spurs? Luckily, my dog followed me. So I placed a message around his neck and sent him home. When my wife saw the note she sent the dog back, carrying the spurs around its neck! Then I was finally able to go. But I never made it to Concord because the British captured me! At last they freed me, but they wouldn't give me back my horse!

Revere 2: Actually, I never rode at all that night. I was just too tired to go the twelve miles to Concord. Instead, I sent homing pigeons that I'd raised for just that purpose. I attached a small message to each one's wings, and they were off! They knew exactly where to go.

Revere 3: I didn't need to go anywhere because my fellow patriots and I made up a code. If I hung two lanterns from Christ Church, it meant the British were coming by water. One lantern meant they were coming by land. Everyone for miles around knew the signals, including Sam Adams and John Hancock. They just watched for the signals from where they were.

Host: Okay, everyone. It is now time to decide who you think is the real Paul Revere. With a show of hands, how many think it is Revere 1? *(pause)* Revere 2? *(pause)* Revere 3? *(pause)* Now that everyone has voted, let's have the real Paul Revere please stand up.

PAUL REVERE (1735-1818)

Will the Real Paul Revere Please Stand Up?

☆ Teacher's Page ☆

Who Is the Real Paul Revere?

Once all the votes have been cast, establish that Paul Revere 1 is the real Revere. Then review the play, making sure that students can distinguish all of these true and false statements:

Panelists 1 and 2: All responses to the questions are true.

Panelist 3: Reveres 1 and 2 are telling the truth. But the expression "born with a silver spoon in one's mouth" is just a cliche. No one really made silver spoons for that purpose!

Panelist 4: Again, Revere 3 is the only one not telling the truth. During this time period, Paul Revere would have been boycotting British tea, so he wouldn't have drunk it. In any case, tea bags were not introduced in the United States until the twentieth century. (Supposedly, they evolved from the small silk bags sent as samples to prospective purchasers.)

Panelist 5: In this case, both Reveres 2 and 3 are lying, as there is no question that Revere went on that now-famous ride. (Homing pigeons have been used in communication since ancient times, but they weren't used by Paul Revere!) And the lanterns hung from Christ Church would never have been spotted as far away as Lexington and Concord! This signal was used so that Revere's friends in Charlestown would know to have a horse waiting there for him.

Questions for Discussion

1. Compare how Paul Revere and his classmates were disciplined and rewarded with the way that it is done in classrooms today.

2. Why do you think the British soldiers treated the colonists as they did during the French and Indian War? Do you think there was anything that the colonists could have done to avoid or change this treatment? If so, what might it have been? If not, why is that?

3. Compare the way the colonists protested during the Boston Massacre with their actions at the Boston Tea Party. What else might they have done in each case? Which method(s) of protest do you think are the best? Why?

Activities

1. Research and play games that were popular in colonial times, such as blindman's buff, leapfrog, hopscotch, marbles, and London Bridge. Then compare these with games that are popular today.

2. In colonial days, town criers called people together to read important news announcements aloud. In a paragraph, jot down what a town crier from Boston might have shouted the day after the Boston Massacre or the Boston Tea Party.

3. During their tea boycott, colonists would often brew up their own "liberty teas" to take the place of the real thing. To make liberty tea for your own class, pour hot water over a cup of dried raspberry or strawberry leaves. Once the mixture cools, pour small servings of it into cups, straining the leaves as much as possible.

Will the Real Dolley Madison Please Stand Up?

☆ Characters ☆

Host	Panelist 1
Biographer 1	Panelist 2
Biographer 2	Panelist 3
Madison 1	Panelist 4
Madison 2	Panelist 5
Madison 3	

Host: Welcome to *To Tell the Truth*! Today's guest is Dolley Madison, wife of America's fourth president, James Madison. Only one of our three guests is the real Dolley Madison. The other two are impostors. Listen carefully to what each one says. Then it's up to you to figure out who's telling the truth, the whole truth, and nothing but the truth. Let's begin by meeting our guests.

Madison 1: Hello, everyone. So nice of you to have me here today. My name is Dolley Madison.

Madison 2: Best wishes to all of you. My name is Dolley Madison.

Madison 3: It's lovely to be here today. My name is Dolley Madison.

Biographer 1: Before we start, the real Dolley Madison has asked us to read this letter of introduction to you:

Dear Students: I, Dolley Payne Todd Madison was born in 1768 in Guilford, North Carolina. Soon afterward, my family moved to Virginia. But when I was about fifteen, we moved again to Philadelphia, where I later met my first husband, John Todd, Jr. Not long after that, a terrible yellow fever epidemic swept our area. It claimed the lives of many people, including my husband and one of my two sons. About a year later, I remarried. My second husband, James Madison, went on to become the fourth president of the United States.

Biographer 2: *(continues reading the letter)*

People say that I was in my glory once I became "lady presidentress." I loved entertaining and was constantly opening the President's House to the public. (This was before it became known as "The White House.") I knew eleven presidents in my lifetime. When I died in 1849, President Zachary Taylor dubbed me "the first lady for half a century." That was the first time the phrase "first lady" was ever used to describe the president's wife. And, as I'm sure you know, it is still used today. Signed, Dolley Madison.

Host: Let's begin the questioning with Panelist 1.

Panelist 1: As a person who loved parties and socializing, it must have been difficult for you to be raised a Quaker. Your religion frowned on dancing, singing, and wearing ornaments like buckles and ribbons. The Quakers were also against war and fighting of any kind—including the American Revolution. Some, who didn't understand your religious beliefs, even accused your family of siding with the British during the War for Independence. But that was untrue. What else do you remember about growing up a Quaker?

Madison 1: One night I remember going out to the slave quarters to listen to music. My father found me there, dancing and singing as a fiddler played. Being a strict Quaker, he took me back to the house and gave me a spanking. Then he locked me in my room!

Madison 2: My grandmother who wasn't a Quaker once gave me a beautiful piece of jewelry. I pinned it underneath my dress so no one could see it. But I knew it was there, and it made me feel special. Then one day I discovered that the pin had fallen off. It was gone! I was so upset because I thought I was being punished for wearing something that I wasn't supposed to wear.

Madison 3: Although Quakers were opposed to slavery, Virginia law did not give people permission to free their slaves, legally, until 1782. That year my family was one of the first to let their slaves go. My nanny, Mother Amy, had been one of those slaves. But even after she was freed, she chose to stay with our family.

Panelist 2: As a girl, you loved to ride in the woods and watch people pass by. What else do you remember about your childhood?

Madison 1: I was fortunate enough to go to school, where I learned reading and writing. Math, however, was usually only taught to boys. On my first day, Mother covered me from head to toe so I wouldn't get freckled by the sun. I wore a big bonnet, gloves, and a piece of cloth that covered most of my face! I must have been quite a sight!

Madison 2: When I was twelve, I made my first trifle cake. It was a sponge cake made in three layers. My father thought my mother had baked it because it tasted so good. So I guess it's not too surprising that later in life I became famous for my desserts. In fact, there is a company today that makes cookies and donuts and goes by my name!

Madison 3: Did you know that in my day, people believed that eating fresh fruit could cause diseases? It was also believed that illnesses were caused by "bad blood." Doctors would "bleed" their patients to rid them of blood to make them better. It's a wonder I lived so long, given some of the notions we had back then!

Panelist 3: While your second husband, James Madison, was Secretary of State, President Jefferson's wife died. From then on, you served as the official hostess at the President's House. So, by the time your husband became President, you were already a pro! When you and President Madison gave dinner parties, he would ask you to sit at the head of the table. That way he wouldn't have to lead the conversations. He always felt you were better at this than him. What else did you do as the President's wife?

Madison 1: Whenever we had guests over, I'd carry a book around with me, called *Don Quixote*. It was a great conversation starter!

Madison 2: I popularized ice cream, which wasn't a common dessert at the time, by serving it to my pet macaw on national TV!

Madison 3: I held the first Easter Egg Roll for children on the lawn of the President's House. That custom still continues to this day.

Panelist 4: On August 24, 1814, during the War of 1812, just as you were about to sit down to dinner, word came that the British were planning to attack the capital city. You could hear the gunfire as it got nearer and nearer and you realized that, for your own safety, you would have to leave. Tell us, what happened next?

Madison 1: Well, I wasn't going to do anything until after dinner. But as soon as I finished eating, I disguised myself as a farm woman and quickly got out of town.

Madison 2: Actually, I was captured while I was eating. But I bribed a soldier, who helped me get a message to my husband, telling him what was going on. Troops rushed in to rescue me, just as I was serving the British soldiers a second helping of dessert!

Madison 3: I didn't have time to eat. Before escaping, I quickly packed up whatever important items I could think of, like the Declaration of Independence, the national seal, and a famous painting of George Washington. It's a good thing I did, too. Otherwise, those documents might have been lost forever. Because, after eating the dinner that I'd left, the British wound up torching our house!

Panelist 5: After your husband died, you were honored by Congress in a way that no woman before you ever had been. You were given a permanent seat on the floor of the House of Representatives. What other memories of your later years would you like to share?

Madison 1: Even in my old age I tried to remain a trend-setter. That's why I created the look of wearing high-top sneakers with bell bottom jeans. Is anyone still into that look today?

Madison 2: Sadly, after my husband's death, I used up all my savings on a lifestyle that I couldn't really afford. I wound up having to open up a little bakery, just to make ends meet.

Madison 3: I always remained in the spotlight, almost until my dying day. After Samuel Morse made history by sending out the very first telegram over wires, he invited me to send out the second message. Not knowing what else to do, I sent one to my cousin!

Host: Okay, everyone. It is now time to decide who you think is the real Dolley Madison. With a show of hands, how many think it is Madison 1? *(pause)* Madison 2? *(pause)* Madison 3? *(pause)* Now that everyone has voted, let's have the real Dolley Payne Todd Madison please stand up.

DOLLEY MADISON (1768-1849)

Will the Real Dolley Madison Please Stand Up?
✰ Teacher's Page ✰

Who Is the Real Dolley Madison?

Once all the votes have been cast, establish that Madison 3 is the real Dolley Madison. Then review the play, making sure that students can distinguish all of these true and false statements:

Panelist 1 and 2: All responses to the questions are true.

Panelist 3: As odd as it sounds, both Madisons 1 and 3 are telling the truth here. Though Dolley Madison did popularize ice cream, she obviously didn't do it on TV, which had not been invented yet. (Incidentally, Madison did have a pet macaw. She kept it near a window at the front of her house so children could watch her feed it!)

Panelist 4: Though Madison did disguise herself as a farm woman to make her escape (and she did escape; she was not captured by the British), she did not insist on having her dinner first! Thus only Madison 3 is telling the truth here. (By the way, it was after the presidential mansion was repaired and painted white that it started to be called the White House!)

Panelist 5: Some students may be surprised to learn that jeans and sneakers were not invented until the end of the nineteenth century. And Dolley Madison never went broke and never opened a bakery. Again, only Madison 3 is telling the truth.

Questions for Discussion

1. Based on what you've read here, do you think Dolley Madison was a good "first lady"? Why or why not? Are there any traits that you think it would be helpful for a president's spouse to have?

2. According to the play, Dolley Madison was associated with a lot of famous firsts: the first reference to the presidential home as the White House; the first Easter Egg Roll on the White House lawn; the first ice cream served in the White House; and even the term "first lady" was first used in reference to her! What other famous firsts about the White House would you like to find out about? List them. Then discuss how you might go about researching each one.

3. Dolley Madison used her wits to save some important papers before the British burned down her house during the War of 1812. If you only had a few minutes to save some items from your house, what would you choose to save? Why?

Activities

1. As a class, research Morse Code. Then use it to encode this sentence: "What hath God wrought?" (This was the first message Samuel Morse ever sent over a telegraph wire.) Finally, have students encode their own messages for classmates to decipher.

2. Look up some interesting White House trivia at http://www.whitehouse.gov/WH/kids/html/home.html. Then create a White House Trivia bulletin board display.

3. Write a story about a day in the life of Dolley Madison. In the story, include at least three facts that you learned from the play.

Will the Real Sacagawea Please Stand Up?

☆ Characters ☆

Host	Sacagawea 3
Biographer 1	Panelist 1
Biographer 2	Panelist 2
Biographer 3	Panelist 3
Sacagawea 1	Panelist 4
Sacagawea 2	Panelist 5

* Note that, in other sources you may see Sacagawea's name spelled Sacajawea or Sakakawea. However, this is now the accepted spelling.

Host: Welcome to *To Tell the Truth*! Today's guest is Sacagawea (pronounced Sah-cawg-a-WAY-ah), the Shoshone Indian guide who traveled with Lewis and Clark on their expedition west of the Mississippi. Of course, only one of our three guests is the real Sacagawea. The other two are impostors. Listen carefully to what each one says. Then it's up to you to figure out who's telling the truth, the whole truth, and nothing but the truth. Let's begin by meeting our guests.

Sacagawea 1: Hello. My name is Sacagawea.

Sacagawea 2: Good day, everyone. My name is Sacagawea.

Sacagawea 3: Hello. My name is Sacagawea.

Biographer 1: Before we start, the real Sacagawea has asked us to read this letter of introduction to you:

> Dear Students: I, Sacagawea, was born around 1787 in the area now called "Idaho," in the Rocky Mountains. There were only thirteen states and about four million people in the country then. A few years later, in 1804, Thomas Jefferson, hired Meriwether Lewis and Captain William Clark to find a direct water route west to the Pacific Ocean. At about the same time, the United States signed the Louisiana Purchase agreement with France. This purchase expanded this country's borders. It also calmed any fears that France would try to build an empire on American soil.

Biographer 2: *(continues reading the letter)*

Lewis and Clark hired my husband, a French Canadian trader named Touissant Charbonneau as an interpreter. He asked if I could come along. Lewis and Clark liked the idea—especially since I spoke several Native languages. Besides, we'd be traveling through Shoshone country, where I was born. And, as a Native woman with an infant, I would be a sign to tribe leaders that our expedition had come in peace.

Biographer 3: *(continues reading the letter)*

There are very few records about what happened to me after the expedition. Some say I died in my twenties from a fever. Others say that I lived to be almost one hundred years old. No one knows for sure. All around this country, mountain peaks, creeks, lakes, a mountain pass, and monuments are named for me. I am even honored on a U.S. dollar coin. It is said that no other American woman has as many memorials dedicated to her as I do. Signed, Sacagawea.

Host: Let's begin the questioning with Panelist 1.

Panelist 1: In winter, your people, the Shoshone, lived in tepees on a high plateau in the Rocky Mountains. Then, in spring, the tribe would travel the Great Plains in search of buffalo. They were constantly at battle with another tribe, called the Minnetarees. Tell us some stories about your childhood with your tribe.

Sacagawea 1: First of all, I did not get the name Sacagawea until I was older and had been separated from my tribe. Actually, because of Shoshone traditions, I probably had several different names while I was growing up.

Sacagawea 2: As a girl, my mother would have me watch my baby brother. One day, I placed him in his cradle board, and set it down near the river. But a dog accidentally knocked the cradle board into the water—with my brother in it! Before the currents could carry him downstream, I jumped in and grabbed him. We were both rescued, but it was a close call!

Sacagawea 3: One time my grandmother and I were out looking for firewood in a rocky area. Suddenly, she fell and injured her leg. Just then, a rattlesnake came out from among the rocks and moved toward her. I could see that she was having trouble getting up, so I grabbed a stone and threw it at the snake's head. Then I used my knife to jab it a few times until it was dead.

Panelist 2: When you were about twelve years old, you were captured by the Minnetarees. They're the ones who gave you the name that we know you by today. Tell us something else about your life with them.

Sacagawea 1: Unlike the Shoshone, the Minnetarees were farmers. While living with them, I learned how to hoe the earth and plant seeds for crops like maize, which you call "corn." I also learned other skills, like how to make robes out of buffalo skins and moccasins from the hides of antelope and deer.

Sacagawea 2: More than once, I thought about running away and trying to return to my people. But it would have been a long journey. We traveled about five hundred miles or so after the Minnetarees captured me. I didn't even know if anyone else in my family had survived their raid. So, even though I once had a chance to escape with two other girls from my tribe, I decided to stay behind.

Sacagawea 3: When I was about fifteen years old, a French Canadian trader named Toussaint Charbonneau came to our Minnetaree village and won me in a gambling game. That's how I became his wife.

Panelist 3: Right about the same time that you met Charbonneau, Lewis and Clark were setting out on their expedition. But to cross the Rocky Mountains, they knew they would need horses, supplies, and experienced people like you to help. That's why, even though you had a newborn baby at the time, they allowed you to come along. Tell us, what did you do on the expedition?

Sacagawea 1: On the journey, we faced sickness, hunger, terrible winter months, mosquitoes, and grizzly bears. But on the way, I proved very helpful. I cooked, mended clothes, made hundreds of moccasins for the men, and cared for the sick. I also found roots and berries for us to eat when food was scarce.

Sacagawea 2: Though the men had thought to bring a medicine chest on the trip, there was no doctor. Luckily, my mother and grandmother had taught me how to use herbs and remedies to make people well.

Sacagawea 3: Once, as we were sailing down a river in bad weather, our boat almost capsized. While the others worked to prevent the boat from sinking, I reached over the side and rescued many papers, instruments, and medical supplies that had fallen out. Without these things, we might have had to turn back. In any case, all records of what we'd seen so far would have been lost!

Panelist 4: As you traveled, you started to recognize landmarks and other familiar sights from your childhood. It crossed your mind that you might even see your own people, the Shoshone, on the trip. Then Lewis and Clark brought you, as their interpreter, to a tribe leader. When you realized it was your brother, you were overcome with joy! What did you do then?

Sacagawea 1: What would you have done if you had been kidnapped, made a slave, and then forced to marry a man three times older than you were? I didn't have to think twice! I stayed with the Shoshone.

Sacagawea 2: At first, I didn't think my husband would let me stay. But my brother, as the head of our tribe, agreed to pay a high price for me. So, as it turned out, I was bought back by my people.

Sacagawea 3: This was a hard decision for me. But in the end I decided to continue the journey with the white men. I was curious to see the "great water where the sun set," known as the "Pacific Ocean." Besides, the expedition really seemed to need my help.

Panelist 5: In 1906, when the Lewis and Clark expedition ended, your husband received $500.33 from the U.S. government for his services. What did you get?

Sacagawea 1: Because I stayed with the Shoshone, I was told that I didn't deserve a thing.

Sacagawea 2: I was awarded the exact same amount of money as my husband. After all, that was only fair.

Sacagawea 3: I received no money from the government, as they saw me as nothing more than Charbonneau's wife. But Captain Clark, who had become very attached to my son, Jean Baptiste, offered to pay for his education, which he later did. My son was thus raised as a white man, and later became the mayor of San Luis Rey, California.

Host: Okay, everyone. It is now time to decide who you think is the real Sacagawea. With a show of hands, how many think it is Sacagawea 1? *(pause)* Sacagawea 2? *(pause)* Sacagawea 3? *(pause)* Now that everyone has voted, let's have the real Sacagawea please stand up.

Will the Real Sacagawea Please Stand Up?
☆ Teacher's Page ☆

Who Is the Real Sacagawea?

Once all the votes have been cast, establish that Sacagawea 3 is the real Sacagawea. Then review the play, making sure that students can distinguish all of these true and false statements:

Panelists 1, 2, and 3: All responses to the questions are true.

Panelist 4: Surprising as it is, from the records that were kept, it doesn't seem that Sacagawea even considered staying with her brother. Thus, only Sacagawea 3 is telling the truth.

Panelist 5: Again, only Sacagawea 3 is telling the truth here.

Questions for Discussion

1. When Sacagawea was taken from her family by the Minnetarees, she did not speak their language nor understand their customs. Even the foods they ate and the way they cooked were different from what she had always known. (Remember: The Shoshone were nomads who did not stay in one place for long, while the Minnetarees were farmers who did.) What do you think it would be like to suddenly be kidnapped and raised by people whose ways are so drastically different from yours? If you had been Sacagawea, would you have tried to escape? Why or why not?

2. Imagine taking a long journey on foot and by boat, carrying a newborn infant the whole way, as Sacagawea did. What types of hardships do you imagine she experienced on her trip?

3. Are you surprised that Sacagawea did not stay with her Shoshone family when she found them while heading west with Lewis and Clark? Why do you think she chose not to stay?

Activities

1. Using a map of the United States, trace the route of Lewis and Clark's expedition. Then research the geography of these areas. When you're done, describe in a paragraph some of the struggles with nature that the travelers probably had to deal with.

2. Imagine that you were going to be traveling with the Lewis and Clark expedition. What kinds of things would you take with you? Draw a picture of a knapsack. Then fill it with ten items that you would take on the trip. (Tip: You'll probably want to pack light!)

3. Select one incident that occurred on Lewis and Clark's expedition. Then write a diary entry about it from Sacagawea's point of view.

Will the Real Abraham Lincoln Please Stand Up?

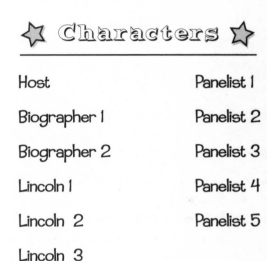

☆ Characters ☆

Host	Panelist 1
Biographer 1	Panelist 2
Biographer 2	Panelist 3
Lincoln 1	Panelist 4
Lincoln 2	Panelist 5
Lincoln 3	

Host: Welcome to *To Tell the Truth*! Today's guest is "Honest Abe" Lincoln, president of the United States during the Civil War. Of course, only one of our three guests is the real Abraham Lincoln. The other two are impostors. Listen carefully to what each one says. Then it's up to you to figure out who's telling the truth, the whole truth, and nothing but the truth. Let's begin by meeting our guests.

Lincoln 1: Hello. My name is Abraham Lincoln. It is an honor to be here today.

Lincoln 2: Honest Abe, that's me. I was the sixteenth president of the United States. Glad to meet you.

Lincoln 3: Greetings, students. I am President Abraham Lincoln.

Biographer 1: Before we start, the real Abraham Lincoln has asked us to read this letter of introduction to you:

> Dear Students: I, Abraham Lincoln, was born in 1809 to a poor family in western Kentucky. While I was still a boy, we moved to Indiana, and then to Illinois. Later, I served as the nation's sixteenth president during a terrible time in our history—the Civil War. When I took the oath of office, I promised to "preserve, protect, and defend" the country. I greatly opposed slavery. But I was even more worried that the war over slavery was tearing our country apart.

Biographer 2: *(continues reading the letter)*

> Even so, in 1863, with the war still raging, I officially freed all slaves with a document known as the Emancipation Proclamation. Later that year, in the Gettysburg Address, I pronounced that "government of the people, by the people, and for the people shall not perish from the earth." On April 9, 1865, the Civil War ended. Five days later, I became the first U.S. president to be assassinated. I was fifty-six years old. Signed, Abraham Lincoln.

Host: Let's begin the questioning with Panelist 1.

Panelist 1: From the day you learned to read, you were an avid bookworm. This frustrated your father, who didn't believe that reading was as important as working in the fields. Then your mother died when you were only nine years old. Life must have been pretty lonely then. What else can you tell us about your childhood?

Lincoln 1: After my mother died, my twelve-year-old sister, Sarah, took on the cooking and cleaning. I guess she even helped raise me a bit. About a year later, my father was remarried to a widow named Sarah Bush Johnson. I loved my new stepmother. And even though she couldn't read herself, she always encouraged me to continue my education.

Lincoln 2: My stepmother used to tease me by saying that, since I was so tall, I'd better keep my hair clean. She didn't want me to dirty up her ceiling. So as a joke, I had a young child step in mud. Then I held him upside down so he could track footprints on the ceiling. My stepmother laughed at that. But I still had to clean up the mess!

Lincoln 3: "My best friend is the man who'll give me a book I haven't read," I used to say. I would walk for miles to borrow one. Once I borrowed a book about George Washington that I really liked. But when I carelessly left it out in the rain, it was ruined. I put in three days of work to pay off the owner for that book. When I was done, he told me to keep it.

Panelist 2: You were born and raised in a one-room log cabin, and you attended a one-room log cabin school. It was called a "blab" school because you were supposed to read your lessons out loud to prove that you were studying. Students who didn't were thought to be lazy and were punished. What else do you remember about school?

Lincoln 1: I guess you could say I "learned by littles." That is, I only went to school when I wasn't needed to do chores. Usually that was just for a few months each winter. My sister and I would walk two miles to get to school, then two miles back. If you totaled up all the days I ever spent there, it would probably add up to about one year.

Lincoln 2: Since paper was expensive, I would practice my writing and spelling in snow, dirt, or dust. Anything! I didn't care! On Fridays at school there was always a spelling bee. The winner was allowed to take a book home for the weekend. So I always tried to win—except once. That day, I helped a girl that I liked spell a word correctly. When the teacher wasn't looking, I pointed to my eye to hint that the next letter in the word was "i." That week, I was happy when the two of us tied for first place!

Lincoln 3: Once I saw some mean kids at school abuse a turtle by placing hot coals on its back. That led me to write a school composition about cruelty to animals. In it I said, "All living things have a right to be treated fairly." I believed that so strongly that sometimes I'd stand up on a tree stump and give talks on the topic.

Panelist 3: You really seemed to earn the nickname "Honest Abe." Once, you walked ten miles to give a woman an item that she had accidentally left at a store where you were working. Another time, after a customer was overcharged by accident, you walked three miles to return the money. That's a lot of walking! Did you do any other traveling as a young man?

Lincoln 1: At nineteen, I was hired to take a flatbed boat down the Ohio and Mississippi rivers to New Orleans. It was my first trip away from home. I'll never forget the slave auctions that I saw on that trip. It was horrible watching people chained up and beaten. I earned $25 for doing that job. But, as was the custom, I had to turn all my earnings over to my father. I resented this, though, as he and I didn't get along well.

Lincoln 2: In 1832, a Native American chief named Black Hawk led one thousand warriors to Illinois to fight the militia and U.S. soldiers. I enlisted to help crush the rebellion. I served a total of eighty days, and for that I was paid $95. But in that time, I also learned a good deal about the life that volunteer soldiers led.

Lincoln 3: In 1836, I opened a law office in Springfield, Illinois. In those days, lawyers like myself would sometimes have to travel around the state to try cases. I usually accompanied Judge David Davis. And sometimes, if he wasn't feeling well, I would act as the judge in his place!

Panelist 4: In 1858, as a candidate for a seat in the Senate, you took part in a series of debates with your opponent Stephen Douglas. In the debates, you told the nation that you thought slavery was wrong. Though you lost that election, you beat Douglas two years later in the race for president. But that led many Southern states that didn't like your anti-slavery beliefs to secede from the Union. By April 1861, about a month after you were sworn into office, the Civil War began. Tell us more about your presidency and the war.

Lincoln 1: The South had a great general named Robert E. Lee. For a while, it looked like the North didn't stand a chance against him. But then I decided to use my height to my advantage. I joined the Union Army as a soldier. Since I could see over just about everybody's heads, I was able to warn my soldiers when the Confederates were approaching. Before long, the North had won!

Lincoln 2: The bloodiest battle of the war took place in Gettysburg, Pennsylvania. Within three days over twenty thousand men had been killed or wounded on each side. A few months later, I participated in a ceremony to dedicate the area as a national cemetery. Soldiers from both the North and the South who had fought one another to the death, would now be buried here together, forever. That's where I gave my famous speech, the Gettysburg Address.

Lincoln 3: As you probably know, CNN did a really fantastic job of reporting the war. Every day, there were on-the-spot interviews at all the major battlefields. These began on April 12, 1860, the day the Confederates first opened fire at Fort Sumter. And they continued until Robert E. Lee surrendered at the Appomattox Courthouse on April 9, 1865.

Panelist 5: Shortly before your assassination, you reported having a very disturbing dream. In it you saw people in the White House crying over a body on a platform with soldiers standing guard. It was your body. In reality you were shot on April 14, 1865, and you died the next morning. What exactly happened, Mr. President?

Lincoln 1: I had always loved acting, and had agreed to appear in the play at Ford's Theater. John Wilkes Booth, a fellow actor, was mad that he hadn't gotten the part. He was sitting in the audience that night and, when he saw me in the role, he pulled out a gun and shot me on the stage.

Lincoln 2: I was sitting in the balcony of Ford's Theater with my wife, Mary, and some of our friends, when John Wilkes Booth snuck in and shot me from behind. He was a Southerner who hated me for my position on slavery. After shooting me, he jumped on the stage to make his get-away. But he didn't get far. While jumping, he injured his leg. Later he was found dead in a barn with a gun. No one knows to this day whether he shot himself or not.

Lincoln 3: John Wilkes Booth was both an actor in the play and a Confederate sympathizer who hated that the North had won the war. In the play, there was a scene where he had to shoot off a gun. So he loaded a real gun with bullets and shot me from the stage. Then he ran off and disappeared. He was never seen or heard from again.

Host: Okay, everyone. It is now time to decide who you think is the real Abraham Lincoln. With a show of hands, how many think it is Lincoln 1? *(pause)* Lincoln 2? *(pause)* Lincoln 3? *(pause)* Now that everyone has voted, let's have the real Abraham Lincoln please stand up.

ABRAHAM LINCOLN (1802-1865)

Will the Real Abraham Lincoln Please Stand Up?
✫ Teacher's Page ✫

Who Is the Real Abraham Lincoln?

Once all the votes have been cast, establish that Lincoln 2 is the real Abraham Lincoln. Then review the play, making sure that students can distinguish all of these true and false statements:

Panelists 1, 2, and 3: All responses to the questions are true.

Panelist 4: The answers that Lincoln 1 and 3 give here are both silly. Aside from the fact that it is rare for the leader of a nation to go into battle, Lincoln's height would only be of limited help on the battlefields. And, obviously, CNN (much less, television) was not yet invented. (However, the Civil War was the first war ever photographed and was quite well covered, journalistically.) Thus, Lincoln 1 and 3 cannot be the real "Honest Abe."

Panelist 5: John Wilkes Booth was indeed both an actor and a Confederate sympathizer. He shot Lincoln, attacking him from behind. Again, Lincoln 2 is the only one telling the whole truth here.

Questions for Discussion

1. Compare the school that Abraham Lincoln attended with the one that you go to. Which one sounds like more fun to you?

2. "Honest Abe" walked many miles to return things that didn't belong to him. What would you have done if you were in his shoes?

3. In some ways, Abraham Lincoln both started the Civil War and ended it. Give specific examples showing how he did each.

4. Why do you think Abraham Lincoln did not wish to punish the South after the war ended? If you were a Northerner, would you have agreed with him on this? Why or why not?

Activities

1. Write a "what if" story about what life might have been like today, if the Confederate Army had won the Civil War.

2. Write a "what if" story about what might have happened if Abraham Lincoln had lived to serve out his second term in office.

3. The Civil War was the first time that photography was used to capture battle scenes in action. Using photographs from newspapers and magazines, create a poster collage about how terrible war can be.

Will the Real Susan B. Anthony Please Stand Up?

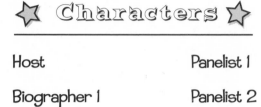

☆ **Characters** ☆

Host	Panelist 1
Biographer 1	Panelist 2
Biographer 2	Panelist 3
Anthony 1	Panelist 4
Anthony 2	Panelist 5
Anthony 3	

Host: Welcome to *To Tell the Truth*! Today's guest is Susan B. Anthony, a crusader in the fight for women's rights. Of course, only one of our three guests is the real Susan B. Anthony. The other two are impostors. Listen carefully to what each one says. Then it's up to you to figure out who's telling the truth, the whole truth, and nothing but the truth. Let's begin by meeting our guests.

Anthony 1: Good day, everyone. My name is Susan B. Anthony.

Anthony 2: Hey, vote for me! I'm the real Susan B. Anthony!

Anthony 3: Greetings, all. My name is Susan B. Anthony.

Biographer 1: Before we start, the real Susan B. Anthony has asked us to read this letter of introduction to you:

Dear Students: I, Susan Brownell Anthony, was born on February 15, 1820, in Adams, Massachusetts. I was the second-oldest of eight children. As a Quaker, my father became very involved in our country's anti-slavery movement. So did I. We both also supported Prohibition, a movement to ban the use of alcohol. Unlike others at that time, my father was a firm believer that girls and boys deserved an equal education. When I was old enough, he sent me to one of the few colleges that would accept women back then.

Biographer 2: *(continues reading the letter)*

More and more, I came to see how much this country discriminated against women. When I went into the workforce, I was paid less than men were. I was told that it wasn't lady like to speak out on issues in which I believed. I wasn't even allowed to vote! So I started to fight harder for women's rights. Some even called me the "Moses of her sex." But I didn't want praise; I wanted justice. Though the Nineteenth Amendment to the U.S. Constitution finally gave women the right to vote in 1920, I didn't live to see it. I died in 1906 at the age of eighty-six. Signed, Susan B. Anthony.

Host: Let's begin the questioning with Panelist 1.

Panelist 1: You learned to read at home when you were only about three years old. Then, when you got older, you started school. But your father pulled you out when the teacher refused to teach you and the other girls long division. Soon after that, he started his own school, run by a teacher he hired named Mary Perkins. She was a wonderful role-model of how strong, capable, and independent a woman could be. What else do you remember about your childhood?

Anthony 1: Back at that first school, I had to sit in the back of the room, away from the teacher's lessons and the stove that kept the room warm. When the long division lessons were given, I'd pretend I was cold and would come up front to try and follow them. But the teacher said that I shouldn't worry my "pretty little head" about long division. That's when my father pulled us out of that school!

Anthony 2: Though you could say that my father was a feminist for his time, he was also a product of his era. When I was about eleven years old, I visited his cotton factory. I saw that whenever yarn became tangled in the machinery there, the foreman called a woman over for help. So I asked my father why he didn't just hire a woman to be in charge. But even he didn't believe it was proper to put a female in that kind of role!

Anthony 3: As a girl, I never felt very pretty—especially because I had crossed eyes. Then, after a doctor tried to correct them, one eye still stayed to the left! So I started hiding my eyes behind glasses, which I really didn't need. If you see a photograph of me, it's probably a side-view, taken from the right. I took pictures that way on purpose because that's my best side!

Panelist 2: At age fifteen, you became a teacher. You earned $2.50 a week. When you left to go back to school, a young man replaced you. Later you found out that he was paid $10 per week for the same job! What other things like that happened that made you mad?

Anthony 1: As a teacher, I started to attend teachers' union meetings. I was outraged when the female teachers, including myself, were told to sit quietly in the back of the room and not contribute ideas. Well, I wouldn't stand for that! "Do you not see," I told them, "that so long as society says a woman has not brains enough to be a doctor, lawyer, or minister, but has plenty to be a teacher, every man of you who [decides] to teach tacitly admits . . . that he has no more brains than a woman?"

Anthony 2: As a Quaker, my father didn't believe there should be singing in our house. But I also knew that my mother, who wasn't raised a Quaker, loved to sing as a girl. When I asked my mom why she didn't sing to my little brother, she said it was because my father didn't want her to. My sister explained that, by law, husbands had the right to make the rules in the home. I thought that was a terrible law, and I wanted to see it changed.

Anthony 3: During the Panic of 1837, my Dad was forced to sell most of his possessions to pay the bills. He sold my mother's things, too, including some of her clothes and wedding gifts. Even a pair of my brother's eyeglasses were sold to pay my father's bills! Mom was very sad about all of this, but the laws at the time were very clear: All property in a marriage belonged to the husband. I wanted to change this unfair law, too.

Panelist 3: In 1848, Elizabeth Cady Stanton and Lucretia Mott organized the first Women's Rights Convention in Seneca Falls, New York. Over three hundred people attended, and the Declaration of Women's Rights was drafted there. The document called for women to be able to speak freely, sue for divorce, own property, have equal opportunities in education and professional jobs, and obtain the right to vote. What role did you play at this historic event?

Anthony 1: I gave a speech at the convention, saying that if women didn't get the right to vote, we'd all leave the United States and start our own nation in Greenland. That sure scared the men!

Anthony 2: As the keynote speaker at the convention, I described many of the inequalities women had suffered up to that point. With the camera crews focused on me, I constantly had to remind myself to point my head sideways so the camera would catch my good side.

Anthony 3: The truth is, I wasn't at the convention. My parents and younger sister went, though, and told me all about it. At the time, I was more involved in the temperance movement, also called the fight for Prohibition. It was a few years after the convention, when I was in Seneca Falls to start a branch of the Women's Temperance Society, that I met Elizabeth Cady Stanton. That was when our fifty-year partnership as crusaders for women's rights really began.

Panelist 4: As someone who had always fought against slavery, you were disappointed that women did not win the right to vote, along with blacks, at the end of the Civil War. Tell us about your famous attempt to vote that led to your arrest.

Anthony 1: It was during the presidential election of 1872. Fifteen other women and I were handcuffed and dragged down to police headquarters for trying to vote in Rochester, New York. Our candidate was Victoria Woodhull, the first woman to run for the office of President of the United States.

Anthony 2: I was arrested because I forgot to bring identification with me when I went downtown to cast my ballot. I insisted that they let me in anyway, but they refused. Then they called the police because they thought that I would become violent.

Anthony 3: Several other women and I tried to prove that the Fourteenth and Fifteenth Amendments to the U.S. Constitution, which gave black males the right to vote, should apply to women, too. On Election Day, 1872, I cast my vote for Ulysses S. Grant. But two weeks later I was arrested at my home. Though I was later found guilty, the judge never forced me to pay the $100 fine. If he had, I would have appealed my case to the Supreme Court!

Panelist 5: In 1868, you and Elizabeth Cady Stanton started a radical weekly newspaper called *The Revolution*. In it you championed women's causes and others in which you believed. The next year, you, Stanton, and Lucretia Mott started the National Woman Suffrage Association. It became well known, though some left to join a competing group, the American Woman Suffrage Association. This organization was more conservative than yours and allowed men to join, which yours didn't. Tell us more about yourself.

Anthony 1: Because of the strides I made for women's rights, the newspapers of my day nick-named me "the Martin Luther King, Jr., of the Women's Rights Movement." I always got a kick out of that!

Anthony 2: In 1921, Adelaide Johnson built a sculpture of three famous feminists—Elizabeth Cady Stanton, Gloria Steinem, and myself. But anti-feminists threw so many rotten eggs and tomatoes at it, it was eventually taken down. Today it sits, forgotten, in the basement of the Capitol.

Anthony 3: Have you ever seen a Susan B. Anthony silver dollar? I was the first woman to ever have her face featured on a U.S. coin!

Host: Okay, everyone. It is now time to decide who you think is the real Susan B. Anthony. With a show of hands, how many think it is Anthony 1? *(pause)* Anthony 2? *(pause)* Anthony 3? *(pause)* Now that everyone has voted, let's have the real Susan B. Anthony please stand up.

Will the Real Susan B. Anthony Please Stand Up?
☆ Teacher's Page ☆

Who Is the Real Susan B. Anthony?

Once all the votes have been cast, establish that Anthony 3 is the real Susan B. Anthony. Then review the play, making sure that students can distinguish all of these true and false statements:

Panelists 1 and 2: All responses to the questions are true.

Panelist 3: Students may be surprised to learn that Susan B. Anthony did not attend the famous Seneca Falls Convention. Thus, only Anthony 3 is telling the truth here.

Panelist 4: Victoria Woodhull did run for president in 1872, but Anthony did not vote for her. Though active for awhile in Anthony's National Woman Suffrage Association, Woodhull's views were far more radical, and she and Anthony eventually parted ways. As far as Anthony 2 goes, there is no reason to arrest a person for not carrying identification. Thus, again, only Anthony 3 is telling the truth here.

Panelist 5: Neither Martin Luther King, Jr., nor Gloria Steinem were born in Susan B. Anthony's lifetime. Instead, Anthony was occasionally referred to as the "Napoleon of the Women's Rights Movement." And, in 1921, Adelaid Johnson did build a sculpture of Anthony, Stanton, and Lucretia Mott. The day after it was dedicated, it was placed in the basement of the Capitol Building! But finally, in 1997, it became the first statue of women to be placed in the rotunda of the Capitol. Again, only Anthony 3 is telling the truth.

Questions for Discussion

1. What do you think it would have been like to be female during Susan B. Anthony's time?

2. Do you think men should have been allowed to join Anthony's National Woman Suffrage Association? Why or why not?

3. Susan B. Anthony did many things in her lifetime to fight for causes that she believed in. What were some of them? How far would you go to fight for something in which you believe?

4. Susan B. Anthony was not allowed to speak in her own defense at the trial in which she was found guilty of voting. If you were her, would you have paid the $100 fine? Why or why not?

Activities

1. Imagine that you were one of Susan B. Anthony's supporters. Create a poster explaining why you think women should have the right to vote.

2. Write a diary entry in which you pretend to be Susan B. Anthony. Explain why you feel so strongly about women's rights.

3. Write a letter to Susan B. Anthony describing how conditions for women have changed since her lifetime.

Will the Real Clara Barton Please Stand Up?

☆ **Characters** ☆

Host	Panelist 1
Biographer 1	Panelist 2
Biographer 2	Panelist 3
Barton 1	Panelist 4
Barton 2	Panelist 5
Barton 3	

Host: Welcome to *To Tell the Truth*! Today's guest is Clara Barton, Civil War nurse and founder of the American Red Cross. Of course, only one of our three guests is the real Clara Barton. The other two are impostors. Listen carefully to what each one says. Then it's up to you to figure out who's telling the truth, the whole truth, and nothing but the truth. Let's begin by meeting our guests.

Barton 1: Good day, students. I am Clara Barton.

Barton 2: It is wonderful to be here today. My name is Clara Barton.

Barton 3: Hi! Is everyone feeling okay? My name is Clara Barton.

Biographer 1: Before we start, the real Clara Barton has asked us to read this letter of introduction to you:

Dear Students: I, Clarissa Harlowe Barton, was born on Christmas day, *1821*, in North Oxford, Massachusetts. My four siblings, all much older than I, nicknamed me "Tot," or "Baby." Later they settled on "Clara," and that stuck. After teaching for a few years, I moved to Washington, D.C., where I became the first female clerk at the U.S. Patent Office. There, in *1861*, I watched wounded Civil War soldiers being brought to town, and I knew that I had to help.

Biographer 2: *(continues reading the letter)*

> It took time, but I finally was granted permission to take my self-taught nursing skills to the battlefield. Then, when the war ended, I began a nationwide search for missing soldiers. Later, on a trip to Europe, I first heard about an organization called the "International Committee of the Red Cross." Back home, I helped to establish an American chapter, and I remained its president until I was eighty-two years old. For nine years after that I remained active until I died of pneumonia at the age of ninety-one. Signed, Clara Barton.

Host: Let's begin the questioning with Panelist 1.

Panelist 1:   When you were about fifteen, you overheard a doctor tell your parents that you had a very sensitive nature. He said, "She will never assert herself for herself; she will suffer wrong first, but for others she will be perfectly fearless." What other memories do you have about growing up?

Barton 1:   I was always extremely shy, almost afraid of my own shadow. But I never wanted anyone to worry about me. One time, when I was very little, I was terrified by a snake. But I was even more upset by the look on my parents' faces when they saw that I might be in danger. I didn't want to cause them any worry, and felt badly that I had.

Barton 2:   As a young girl, I once walked into a barn just as some workers were butchering an ox. When I saw what was happening, I fainted on the spot! Late, I told my parents that I felt as if I, not the animal, had been struck down.

Barton 3:   Christmas gifts in my family were usually practical things like hats, gloves, or shoes. But since my birthday fell on Christmas, I would also get a cake. One year, I remember cutting pieces for everyone—including my dog, Brownie. I was so excited that I forgot to save myself a slice! Of course, almost everyone—except Brownie—offered to share theirs with me.

Panelist 2:   With four older siblings, you sometimes felt like you had six parents. But they all taught you many things. In addition to reading, writing, and math, your brothers and cousins taught you "unladylike" skills like horseback riding and ice skating. How did some of the things you learned as a child help you later in life?

Barton 1:   When I was about eleven, my brother David was seriously injured while helping to build a barn. The doctors warned us that he might not live. For almost two years, I stayed at his bedside nursing him until he got better. Later I often wondered if this was what inspired me to always help others in pain.

Barton 2: At seventeen, I started my first teaching job. I was very nervous. But I soon won my students' respect because my brothers had taught me how to play ball so well! As for my horseback riding skills, they helped me out on the Civil War battlefields. There were times when I'd stay at the frontline until all of the injured soldiers were assisted. Then I'd make a quick getaway on the back of a horse!

Barton 3: With four much older siblings, I was fairly independent—some would even say stubborn— from a very young age. Yet, as the first female clerk in the U.S. Patent Office, these traits came in handy. Many of the men resented my presence. They felt I was taking the job away from a man. One fellow worker even showed his anger by spitting tobacco juice at me! My independence and stubbornness helped me survive the abuse I sometimes had to take on that job.

Panelist 3: Soon after the Civil War began, you left the U.S. Patent Office to help wounded soldiers who were brought back to the capital. But you knew that you could save even more lives closer to the front. For over a year, the military forbade you from going. Battlefields were no place for women and you would just get in the way, they said. But you persisted, rounding up three warehouses full of food and supplies, before the army let you go. Tell us, "Angel of the Battlefield," what horrors of war did you see?

Barton 1: I trudged through mud and worse to get to injured soldiers. At times, I even had to wring blood out from the bottom of my dress before I could walk. And once, a bullet ripped through my sleeve and killed an injured man, just as I leaned over to help him!

Barton 2: At the Battle of Antietam, I met a soldier who was overly shy about getting medical attention. It turned out to be a woman dressed like a man. Hundreds of females disguised as male soldiers fought and died during the Civil War. This particular woman survived her wounds and later named her first child after me.

Barton 3: I put myself in so much danger on the battlefield that it was no great surprise when I was hit by a stray bullet. For many months after that, I lay in bed while soldiers waited on me hand and foot. I was frustrated that I couldn't be of more assistance from then on, but there was really nothing that I could do about it.

Panelist 4: During the war, you often spent your own money on bandages, blankets, and other supplies. You also started a letter-writing campaign, asking others to help. By the war's end, you were so well known that people came to you to help find their loved ones who were missing in action. So you led a search. After four years, you learned what had happened to about 22,000 soldiers. What else did you do after the war?

Barton 1: One day, I received a letter from a former Union soldier named Dorence Atwater. He had been captured and sent to Georgia's Andersonville Prison during the war. There, he was ordered to keep a list of all of the prisoners who died. I helped him to publish the list, which contained over 13,000 names. Later, I also helped turn Andersonville into a national cemetery, which it still is today.

Barton 2: I spent so much of my money trying to help others that, before long, I was nearly broke. So, even though I was very shy in front of an audience, I started traveling the country, giving speeches about my wartime experiences. I earned $75 to $100 per talk, and I'd give as many as fourteen speeches a month.

Barton 3: While on the lecture circuit, I met Elizabeth Cady Stanton and Susan B. Anthony. Like them, I started to speak out for women's rights. I was tired of thinking about the war. It was nice to talk about something else for a change.

Panelist 5: After everything you'd gone through, doctors recommended that you take a vacation. So you went to Europe. On the trip, you met Dr. Louis Appia of the International Red Cross. You had never heard of the organization. But the more you learned about it, the more you liked it. So what did you do next?

Barton 1: While I was in Europe, a war broke out between France and Prussia. I worked with the International Red Cross to help those in need during that war. Then I came back to the United States to convince my country to sign the Treaty of Geneva. That would make the United States part of the International Red Cross, too.

Barton 2: Government leaders in the United States insisted that there was no need for the Red Cross because no war was being fought here. That's when I suggested to Geneva Convention nations that they declare a war if the United States didn't join. That worked. In March 1882, Congress ratified the Treaty of Geneva, and President Chester A. Arthur signed it.

Barton 3: For the next thirteen years, I served as president of the American Red Cross. I even suggested extending the organization so that it didn't just provide aid during wars and other national crises. I believed it should help families with individual problems, too. So I set up a hotline phone number that people with problems could call.

Host: Okay, everyone. It is now time to decide who you think is the real Clara Barton. With a show of hands, how many think it is Barton 1? *(pause)* Barton 2? *(pause)* Barton 3? *(pause)* Now that everyone has voted, let's have the real Clara Barton please stand up.

Will the Real Clara Barton Please Stand Up?
☆ Teacher's Page ☆

Who Is the Real Clara Barton?

Once all the votes have been cast, establish that Barton 1 is the real Clara Barton. Then review the play, making sure that students can distinguish all of these true and false statements:

Panelists 1 and 2: All responses to the questions are true.

Panelist 3: Everything described by Barton 1 and 2 about the war is true. This makes it all the more surprising that, though she did suffer from fatigue and have some narrow escapes, there are no records of Barton ever sustaining serious injuries during the war.

Panelist 4: Everything Barton 1 and 2 say here is true, too. Barton 3 is telling a partial lie. Though she did give talks about feminism along with Elizabeth Cady Stanton and Susan B. Anthony, Barton never stopped speaking about the war. She used her role in it to prove that women were just as capable in all ways as men.

Panelist 5: Clara Barton would never have recommended that the Geneva Convention—an international agreement to protect people during war—declare a war. Thus, this part of Barton 2's statement is false. And Barton 3 can't be telling the whole truth, as there were no telephones in her time. (Actually, after she retired from the Red Cross, Clara Barton started the National First Aid Society. It was an organization to help families with individual crises.)

Questions for Discussion

1. What were some of Clara Barton's best traits? What negative ones did she have?

2. Between the ages of eleven and thirteen, Clara Barton did almost nothing else but care for her injured brother. Can you imagine doing that at your age for someone you love?

3. What are some reasons a woman might disguise herself as a soldier to take part in a war? What do you think that would be like?

4. Clara Barton extended the purpose of the Red Cross so that it would help people devastated by natural disasters (like floods, earthquakes, and large fires) as well as wars. What are some other times when large groups of people might need help?

Activities

1. Write a diary entry as if you were Clara Barton, telling about an experience you had during the Civil War.

2. Pretend you are a reporter interviewing Clara Barton in her old age. What questions would you ask? What answers would she give?

3. The idea for the Red Cross began in Geneva, Switzerland. Take a look at Switzerland's flag. Compare it with the symbol of the Red Cross. How are they alike? How do they differ? Now make up a symbol that you would use if you were starting an organization to help people today.

Will the Real Alexander Graham Bell Please Stand Up?

> Mr. Watson, come here. I want to see you.

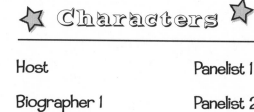

☆ Characters ☆

Host	Panelist 1
Biographer 1	Panelist 2
Biographer 2	Panelist 3
Bell 1	Panelist 4
Bell 2	Panelist 5
Bell 3	

Host: Welcome to *To Tell the Truth*! Today's guest is Alexander Graham Bell, inventor of the telephone and teacher of the deaf. Of course, only one of our three guests is the real Mr. Bell. The other two are impostors. Listen carefully to what each one says. Then it's up to you to figure out who's telling the truth, the whole truth, and nothing but the truth. Let's begin by meeting our guests.

Bell 1: Good day to you all. My name is Alexander Graham Bell.

Bell 2: Did someone ring me? My name is Alexander Graham Bell.

Bell 3: Ahoy, ahoy! My name is Alexander Graham Bell.

Biographer 1: Before we start, the real Mr. Bell has asked us to read this letter of introduction to you:

> Dear Students: I, Alexander Graham Bell, was born on March 3, 1847, in Edinburgh, Scotland. My father and grandfather were both speech teachers and my mother was deaf. Because of these things, I learned the importance of sounds and communication at an early age. I once wanted to be a musician; one of my first jobs was teaching music and speech. But eventually I followed in my father's and grandfather's footsteps, devoting myself to helping the deaf learn to speak.

Biographer 2: *(continues reading the letter)*

In addition to music, I always dabbled in inventing. Like many inventors of my day, I was looking for a way to send more than one message over a telegraph wire at the same time. But while studying this problem, I had another idea: Might it be possible to send the human voice over wires, as well? As it turned out, it was possible. I patented the machine that does it, the telephone, in 1876. When I died in 1922, telephone service in the United States was stopped for one minute in my memory. Signed, Alexander Graham Bell.

Host: Let's begin the questioning with Panelist 1.

Panelist 1: Not only did you share a profession with your father and grandfather, you shared the same name with them, too. When you were eleven, to distinguish yourself from them, you chose the middle name "Graham," after a close family friend. Please tell us more about your childhood, Mr. Bell.

Bell 1: Once my father challenged my brother Melville and I to create a talking robot. So we shaped a head out of wax and a tongue out of stuffed rubber. We made the lips from a piece of wire covered with rubber. Melville made the windpipe using a tin tube and the vocal cords from sheets of tin. Then we used fire bellows for lungs. As my brother worked the bellows, I opened and shut the mouth. The noise that came out sounded like a baby crying. It went, "ma-ma!"

Bell 2: I was so fascinated by sounds that I even tried to teach my dog, Mr. Perd, how to speak. If I pressed my hands against his throat when he growled, I could make it sound as if he was saying, "How are you, Grandma?"

Bell 3: A friend helped me with my first invention when I was only eleven years old. His father, who owned the local mill, challenged us to do something practical—like find a way to remove the husks from grains of wheat. So we did. Using an old barrel with a paddle wheel inside, we cranked out a sack full of wheat in almost no time at all!

Panelist 2: When you were fifteen, you went to live with your grandfather in London. He treated you more like a grown-up than you ever had been at home. So, when you came back to Scotland a year later, you felt much more mature. What other experiences in the years that followed influenced you a great deal?

Bell 1: Before I reached my mid-twenties, both my brothers had died from tuberculosis. That certainly had a big impact on me. Fearing that in Scotland's cold wet climate, I was at risk for the disease too, my parents and I moved to Canada in 1870.

Bell 2: In 1871, my father recommended me for a teaching job at the Boston School for Deaf Mutes, in Massachusetts. I found that I was good at the job. Later I set up a school to train teachers of the deaf. Then I taught at Boston University. From those days on, I always thought of myself first and foremost as a teacher of the deaf.

Bell 3: One of my deaf students was a young woman named Mabel Hubbard. Though I was about ten years older than she was, she and I fell in love. We married on her eighteenth birthday, November 25, 1875.

Panelist 3: That same year, 1875, you hired a young mechanic named Thomas Watson to help you with your experiments. What setbacks, if any, did you have before the telephone was a success?

Bell 1: There were never any setbacks or problems. Everything was smooth sailing from the very first day!

Bell 2: Actually, the invention was not automatically accepted when I introduced it. At first, people just saw it as a "useless toy." I even offered to sell it to Western Union, but they turned me down!

Bell 3: Western Union was sorry, later. They and many others sued me, insisting that they had invented the telephone first. Believe it or not, there were a total of 600 different lawsuits over the telephone! But in the end, I won them all.

Panelist 4: Besides teaching the deaf and inventing the telephone, are there other achievements that you'd like to share with us, sir?

Bell 1: Why? Isn't that enough? I made plenty of money off my invention of the telephone. So, after that, I just decided to retire.

Bell 2: In July, 1881, President James Garfield was shot while walking through a Washington, D.C., railroad station. Doctors couldn't figure out where in his body the bullet was lodged, so I was called in to help. I quickly invented a metal detector that figured out where the bullet was, and I saved the president's life.

Bell 3: My third child, Edward, was born with weak lungs and died within a few hours of his birth. This inspired me to create a machine that could help people with weak lungs breathe easier. Later, others improved on my "vacuum jacket" and renamed it "the iron lung."

Panelist 5: You once said, "It will be possible in a very few years for a person to take his dinner in New York at seven or eight o'clock in the evening and eat his breakfast in either Ireland or England the following morning." This is now the case, but you didn't live to see it happen. Is there anything else you wish you could have lived to see?

Bell 1: Yes. I would have liked to see a "heavier than air" machine take flight with a person in it. Can you imagine such a thing?!

Bell 2: I wish I could have been there when a phone call made in New York City could be heard all the way out on the other side of the country, in California. Now that would have been a hoot!

Bell 3: Well, I wish I could have said something a bit more memorable than "Mr. Watson, come here. I want to see you," during that first historic phone call. But I really can't complain. Overall, I would say I had a pretty wonderful life.

Host: Okay, everyone. It is now time to decide who you think is the real Alexander Graham Bell. With a show of hands, how many think it is Bell 1? *(pause)* Bell 2? *(pause)* Bell 3? *(pause)* Now that everyone has voted, let's have the real Alexander Graham Bell please stand up.

Will the Real Alexander Graham Bell Please Stand Up?

☆ Teacher's Page ☆

Who Is the Real Alexander Graham Bell?

Once all the votes have been cast, establish that Bell 3 is the real Alexander Graham Bell. Then review the play, making sure that students can distinguish all of these true and false statements:

Panelists 1 and 2: All responses to the questions are true.

Panelist 3: It would be incredibly rare for the launch of a new invention to take place without any problems. Bell 1's answer must be false, given that Bell 2 and Bell 3 are telling the truth.

Panelist 4: Only Bell 3 is telling the truth here. Alexander Graham Bell did make a great deal of money from his invention of the telephone. But he never truly retired. As for the incident involving President Garfield, Bell was called in to help, but unfortunately, his metal detector was unable to help the President, who died. Later, though, he improved on the invention, and it was successfully used by surgeons until being replaced in 1895 by X-rays.

Panelist 5: Alexander Graham Bell did live to see a "heavier than air" machine take flight with a person in it. (That's why he came to believe that overseas flights would not be far behind.) And he participated in the first transamerican phone call in January 1915, placing the call himself, from New York, to Mr. Watson in California. And, though Mr. Bell did wish that he'd said something a bit more profound the first time his voice came through the wire, he probably would have agreed that, overall, he did have a good life!

Discussion Questions

1. What kinds of skills do you think it takes to be an inventor? What skills does it take to be a teacher of the deaf? Can you think of any skills that it would be useful for both types of people to have?

2. Before Alexander Graham Bell invented the telephone, people couldn't imagine speaking with people on the other side of the country, much less on the other side of the planet! Can you imagine what it was like for this to be a big deal? How might life be different today if there were no such things as telephones or e-mail?

3. Alexander Graham Bell always regretted that his wife could never use the telephone that he invented because she was deaf. What things do you take for granted that you could not do if you were unable to hear?

Activities

1. Create a timeline showing the history of the telephone. Include how the look of the telephone has changed over time.

2. Write a letter to Alexander Graham Bell describing some of the innovations that have taken place in long-distance communication since he died.

3. In 1902, Helen Keller dedicated her autobiography to her good friend Alexander Graham Bell. Imagine that you are Mr. Bell, and write a short autobiography from Bell's point of view. Don't forget to include a dedication to someone!

Will the Real Thomas Alva Edison Please Stand Up?

☆ Characters ☆

Host	Panelist 1
Biographer 1	Panelist 2
Biographer 2	Panelist 3
Biographer 3	Panelist 4
Edison 1	Panelist 5
Edison 2	Panelist 6
Edison 3	

Host: Welcome to *To Tell the Truth*! Today's guest is the well-known inventor, Thomas Alva Edison. Of course, only one of our three guests is the real Thomas Edison. The other two are impostors. Listen carefully to what each one says. Then it's up to you to figure out who's telling the truth, the whole truth, and nothing but the truth. Let's begin by meeting our guests.

Edison 1: Hello. My name is Thomas Edison.

Edison 2: Greetings, everyone. I'm Thomas Edison.

Edison 3: It is a pleasure to be here today. My name is Thomas Edison.

Biographer 1: Before we start, the real Thomas Edison has asked us to read this letter of introduction to you:

Dear Students: I, Thomas Alva Edison, was born in Milan, Ohio, on February 11, 1847. In my life, I patented 1,093 inventions. That's still more than anyone else in history! One reason I may have been so focused is that I was always hard of hearing. It began when I had scarlet fever as a child, and it grew worse as I got older.

Biographer 2: *(continues reading the letter)*

More than just an inventor, though, I was also a businessman. I created the world's first "invention factory," or large-scale industrial research lab. There, experts worked side-by-side, sharing ideas. Back then, this was a new concept. Today, most large corporations rely on research teams like this all the time.

Biographer 3: *(continues reading the letter)*

Let's face it, the world would look pretty different today if it weren't for me. My staff and I created, or improved on, many things that you still use—from lightbulbs and motion pictures to X-rays and alkaline batteries. I was still inventing when I died, at age eighty-four, on October 18, 1931. A few days later, on the night of my funeral, all electricity in the United States was shut off for one full minute in my honor. Signed, Thomas Alva Edison.

Host: Let's begin the questioning with Panelist 1.

Panelist 1: Word has it that you were a precocious child, mature beyond your years. But you were also a prankster, constantly getting into mischief. Can you tell us more about your childhood, Mr. Edison?

Edison 1: Well, I always did take a "hands-on" approach to learning that sometimes got me into trouble. For example, once I wondered if I could hatch eggs like the goose in our barn. So I built my own nest and filled it with eggs to find out. Of course, I wound up with nothing but a very sticky, yellow pair of pants!

Edison 2: I also did something that kids should never do—I experimented with fire. Even worse, I did it in my father's barn. The fire got out of hand, and the barn burned to the ground. My father was so mad, he took me to the town square so that people could watch me get a whipping!

Edison 3: Once I concocted a mixture that I thought would make a person able to fly. Then I convinced my father's hired hand to drink it. But instead of flying, he just got very sick, and a doctor had to be called in.

Panelist 2: Since you were such a curious child, you must have done well in school. Is that true, Mr. Edison? What kind of education did you have growing up?

Edison 1: Actually, I did terribly in school. The teacher, Reverend Engle, wanted me to memorize facts. But I wanted to understand what I was learning. He said that I asked too many questions. Also, I was a big daydreamer. With my hearing problem, I had a hard time paying attention. After three months in the school, my mother decided it would be better to educate me at home.

Edison 2: My parents often read to me out loud. Before I was twelve, I was familiar with the works of Charles Dickens, William Shakespeare, and a huge book, famous at that time, called *The Decline and Fall of the Roman Empire*, by Edward Gibbon.

Edison 3: After a while, I became such an avid reader of science books, my father would sometimes offer me a penny to read anything else. But his idea backfired. Whenever he gave me money, I spent it on materials for my science experiments!

Panelist 3: You set up your first science laboratory in the house when you were about ten years old. Then, when you were twelve, you got a job as a "candy butcher," selling newspapers, fruit, and candy to passengers on the Grand Trunk Railroad. What happened to you after that?

Edison 1: One day, when I was about fifteen, I saw the stationmaster's little boy playing on the tracks. Then I saw a boxcar rolling toward him! I quickly pulled the child out of the way before he could get hurt. In gratitude, his father taught me how to operate a telegraph machine. For the next six years, I traveled around the country, making a living doing just that.

Edison 2: The telegraph was basically the "telephone" of my time. My job was to wait for messages to come in, and then translate them from the dots and dashes of Morse Code. I preferred night jobs, so that I could sleep or do experiments during my shift. But occasionally, I'd get caught. Then it was time to find a new job!

Edison 3: In 1869, I was granted my first patent for an invention. It was an instant vote recorder that I thought the U.S. Congress could use. But as it turned out, congressmen didn't want to vote by machine. They preferred to shout their votes out loud so they could give speeches on their opinions at the same time. It was then that I learned a big lesson about inventing: Only create things that people really want!

Panelist 4: In 1869, you moved to New York City and landed a job in the financial district. Before long, you figured out a way to improve on Wall Street's ticker tape machines. The Western Union Company paid you very well for that idea. Then, with the money you earned, you started your own business. By 1876, you were ready to open a big laboratory in Menlo Park, New Jersey. What bright ideas did you have there, earning you the nickname, "the Wizard of Menlo Park"?

Edison 1: The brightest idea I had was for the electric light bulb, of course. When I started working on it, I thought it would take me no more than six weeks. But, in fact, it took me almost a year.

Edison 2: After inventing moving pictures, it just made sense to come up with a popcorn maker next. After all, what goes better with a good movie then a big tub of popcorn?

Edison 3: While studying Alexander Graham Bell's new invention, the telephone, I figured out a way to record one's voice and then play it back. Of all my inventions, that one—the phonograph—was always my favorite.

Panelist 5: Speaking of the phonograph, do you happen to remember the first message you ever recorded on one?

Edison 1: Sure. I cranked the machine and spoke into the tinfoil on the cylinder this statement: "That's one small step for a man, one giant leap for mankind."

Edison 2: Actually, my first words were "Mr. Watson, come here. I want to see you."

Edison 3: I bent down toward the machine and recited the words to the nursery rhyme, "Mary Had a Little Lamb."

Panelist 6: You often had interesting things to say about hard work and the creative process. For example, you once said, "The more to do, the more done." Another time, you said, "Thinking is a habit. If you don't learn to think when you're young, you may never learn." Do you have other words of wisdom that you'd like to share?

Edison 1: After inventing the lightbulb, I'd walk into a dark room and suggest to people that they "put a little light on the subject." That always got a laugh.

Edison 2: One of the telephone companies uses my favorite expression: "Reach out and touch someone."

Edison 3: I never thought of myself as brilliant. But I was a hard worker. That's why I'm often quoted as saying, "Genius is one percent inspiration and ninety-nine percent perspiration." I always found that to be true of myself.

Host: Okay, everyone. It is now time to decide who you think is the real Thomas Edison. With a show of hands, how many think it is Edison 1? *(pause)* Edison 2? *(pause)* Edison 3? *(pause)* Now that everyone has voted, let's have the real Thomas Edison please stand up.

Will the Real Thomas Alva Edison Please Stand Up?
☆ Teacher's Page ☆

Who Is the Real Thomas Alva Edison?

Once all the votes have been cast, establish that Edison 3 is the real Thomas Edison. Then review the play, making sure that students can distinguish all of these true and false statements:

Panelists 1, 2 and 3: All responses to the questions are true.

Panelist 4: Edison did invent the electric light bulb and the phonograph in Menlo Park, New Jersey. But he had nothing to do with popcorn makers. Only Edison 2 is telling a lie here.

Panelist 5: Astronaut Neil Armstrong said, "That's one small step for a man, one giant leap for mankind," as he took his first steps on the moon. "Mr. Watson, come here. I want to see you," were Alexander Graham Bell's first words into a telephone. Only Edison 3 is telling the truth here.

Panelist 6: Edison 1 and 2 are quoting a figure of speech and an advertising slogan, respectively. Only Edison 3 is truly quoting Edison here.

Questions for Discussion

1. If you had been the first to ever record something on a phonograph, what memorable words might you have chosen to say? Why?

2. Of all Thomas Edison's many inventions, which one do you think was most important? What makes you think so?

3. What do you think Thomas Edison meant when he said, "Genius is one percent inspiration and ninety-nine percent perspiration"? Do you agree with this statement? Why or why not?

Activities

1. Imagine that you have been hired to promote one of Thomas Edison's inventions. Pick one. Then draw an advertisement explaining what the item is, what it does, and why a person should buy it.

2. Do you have an idea for an invention? What is it? In a paragraph, describe what it is, and how it would work. Then draw a picture showing how it would look.

3. After doing some research, draw a picture showing how a city like New York may have looked in 1847, the year Edison was born. Then draw a second picture showing how it might have looked in 1931 when he died. In a paragraph, describe the changes that took place in that time period. What role did Edison play in the transformation?

Will the Real Nellie Bly Please Stand Up?

☆ Characters ☆

Host	Panelist 1
Biographer 1	Panelist 2
Biographer 2	Panelist 3
Bly 1	Panelist 4
Bly 2	Panelist 5
Bly 3	Panelist 6

Host: Welcome to *To Tell the Truth!* Today's guest is Elizabeth Cochran, who achieved fame as a journalist under the pen name "Nellie Bly." Of course, only one of our three guests is the real Nellie Bly. The other two are impostors. Listen carefully to what each one says. Then it's up to you to figure out who's telling the truth, the whole truth, and nothing but the truth. Let's begin by meeting our guests.

Bly 1:   It is truly a privilege to be here today. My name is Nellie Bly.

Bly 2:   Greetings, students. My name is Nellie Bly.

Bly 3:   Hello, everyone. My name is Nellie Bly.

Biographer 1:   Before we start, the real Nellie Bly has asked us to read this letter of introduction to you:

Dear Students: I, Nellie Bly, was born Elizabeth Cochran on May 5, 1864, in Cochran's Mills, Pennsylvania. The town was named after my father, a wealthy judge and businessman. He died when I was six years old, and my mother remarried. But my stepfather was abusive, so she soon filed for divorce. Like other single moms, it was hard for mine to make ends meet. So you can imagine my horror when a local newspaper, the *Pittsburgh Dispatch*, printed an opinion piece arguing that women should stay home and stop taking jobs away from men!

Biographer 2: *(continues reading the letter)*

> Furious, I wrote a letter to the editor. They were so impressed by it that they offered me a job! I was one of the first female journalists in America, and I became well known for my "behind-the-scenes" reporting. I would go to places that the public didn't usually see—like a mental institution or a woman's prison—and describe the conditions there. Later I also made a well-publicized trip around the world in a record-setting 72 days. I died in 1922, when I was about fifty-five years old. Signed, Nellie Bly.

Host: Let's begin the questioning with Panelist 1:

Panelist 1: Seeing what your mother went through, you probably became a feminist at a very young age. Is that true, Ms. Bly? What memories do you have of growing up female in the mid-1800s?

Bly 1: Well, girls in my day were expected to wear starched dresses and act "ladylike." Since my dresses were usually pink, I was nicknamed "Pinky" by my friends.

Bly 2: I remember when I was about eight years old, one of my brothers and I went horse-back riding. Then he challenged me to a race. But when I won, he told me, "Girls aren't supposed to beat boys at anything." Boy, did that make me mad!

Bly 3: When I was a teenager, one of the few jobs open to women was teaching. So I entered a school to learn how to teach. But I had to drop out because I couldn't afford it. It was frustrating seeing how much easier it was for my brothers to find decent jobs than me!

Panelist 2: How did people react when you told them that you were going to be a reporter for the *Pittsburgh Dispatch*?

Bly 1: My brothers and their wives were horrified! They said it was very unladylike to work for a newspaper, and they accused me of embarrassing the family name.

Bly 2: Even newspapers back then wouldn't let women write under their real names. One of the men in the newsroom suggested the pen name Nellie Bly. It came from a Stephen Foster song written before the Civil War. From then on, that was the name I used.

Bly 3: At first, it looked like I might not even be able to take the job. As a female, I needed permission from an older male family member first. And since my brothers didn't like the idea, I thought that they would say no. But my mom was on my side. She pointed out to them that, with the pen name, no one would even know it was me!

Panelist 3: Besides writing about conditions in mental hospitals and prisons, what other kinds of reporting did you do?

Bly 1: The first article I ever did for the *Dispatch* was about how hard it was to be a poor working girl in Pittsburgh. Next I wrote about the problems with Pennsylvania's divorce laws. Both topics were perfect for me, as I knew about them firsthand!

Bly 2: Toward the end of 1886, I went to Mexico to write about political corruption and living conditions of the poor there. As a single woman, people felt that I needed a chaperone, so my mother came along. But Mexican officials were so angered by my articles that they expelled me from the country after only a few months!

Bly 3: I loved to cover events like fashion shows and flower shows. It was fabulous that, with my press pass, I could get into them for free!

Panelist 4: Eventually, you decided that you wanted to make it into the big time, so you went looking for a job in New York. Was it as easy to find one there as you thought it would be?

Bly 1: It sure was. After seeing all the great articles I'd written for the *Dispatch*, every newspaper in the city wanted to hire me!

Bly 2: Actually, it wasn't easy at all. Using my press credentials from the *Dispatch*, I went to every newspaper. I told them that I was writing an article about whether or not a woman could make it as a journalist in New York. But they all told me that the answer was no!

Bly 3: No, it wasn't easy, but I was persistent. I was looking for over six months before the managing editor at Joseph Pulitzer's *New York World* finally made me an offer. He said that if I could get into Blackwell's Island, a women's asylum, and write a story about it from the inside, I could have a job. So that's exactly what I did!

Panelist 5: In 1873, a popular book, *Around the World in 80 Days*, was published. That gave you an idea. You suggested to the *New York World* that you go around the world and try to beat the fictitious record set in that book. What happened next?

Bly 1: The *Daily World* liked the idea, but they wanted to send a man on the assignment. "Very well," I threatened. "Start the man and I'll start the same day for some other newspaper and beat him." With that logic, I convinced them that I was the right one for the job.

Bly 2:   While going through France, I got to meet Jules Verne, the author of *Around the World in 80 Days*. He was excited that I was attempting the adventure described in his book, and he wished me "good duck." (That's how he said it; his English wasn't very good.) Of course, we didn't talk long. I was in a race against the clock!

Bly 3:   With a monkey that I'd bought in Singapore to keep me company, I arrived back in New Jersey seventy two days, six hours, and eleven minutes after I had left there. That was over a week faster than it took Phileas Fogg, the character in Mr. Verne's book!

Panelist 6:   What were some of the biggest problems that you encountered on your journey?

Bly 1:   The biggest problem I had was keeping track of my luggage. It was lost at just about every baggage check area on the trip!

Bly 2:   Just as I was leaving the United States, I found out that Elizabeth Bisland, a reporter for *Cosmopolitan* magazine, was going to race around the world, too. That kept me on my toes! But in the end, I completed my journey four days before her!

Bly 3:   With delays at just about every airport along the way, it's truly amazing that I made it back in time.

Host: Okay, everyone. It is now time to decide who you think is the real Nellie Bly. With a show of hands, how many think it is Bly 1? *(pause)* Bly 2? *(pause)* Bly 3? *(pause)* Now that everyone has voted, let's have the real Nellie Bly please stand up.

Will the Real Nellie Bly Please Stand Up?
☆ Teacher's Page ☆

Who Is the Real Nellie Bly?

Once all the votes have been cast, establish that Bly 2 is the real Nellie Bly. Then review the play, making sure that students can distinguish all of these true and false statements:

Panelists 1 and 2: All responses to the questions are true.

Panelist 3: Although Nellie Bly was forced to cover fashion shows and the like, she wasn't happy being relegated to the women's page. In part, this eventually helped her decide to leave her job at the *Dispatch*. Thus, Bly 3 is not telling the whole truth here.

Panelist 4: Given that Bly 2 and Bly 3 are telling the truth here, Bly 1's statement has to be false.

Panelist 5: All responses to the question are true.

Panelist 6: Only Bly 2 is telling the truth here. The real Nellie Bly took only one piece of hand luggage on her journey. It contained two dresses (one for hot weather and one for cold) and a variety of personal items and writing tools that she would need. And, of course, Bly 3's statement can't be true. Transportation on Bly's actual trip included everything from boats and trains to donkeys, rickshaws, and sampans. But "heavier-than-air flying machines" were not tested until 1896. (Bly's trip began on November 14, 1889.) Obviously, there were no airports back in her day.

Questions for Discussion

1. What do you think it would have been like to grow up female in Nellie Bly's time? How are attitudes about women different today? Can you think of any ways in which they're the same?

2. What types of things do you think Nellie Bly learned as a reporter working "undercover" that she might not have found out otherwise? Why do you think this might be?

3. In Nellie Bly's day, going around the world in less than 80 days was a big deal. Today it can be done in under 24 hours! Can you think of any adventures that are left in the world that have never been done before? List some of them.

4. Nellie Bly was inspired to make a trip around the world because of a book that she'd read. Has a book ever made you want to try something that you've never done before? What was it?

Activities

1. Read the book *Around the World in 80 Days* by Jules Verne. Then write a book report on it.

2. Research the route that Nellie Bly took on her famous trip around the world. Then draw a map showing the route.

3. Imagine that you are Nellie Bly, traveling around the world. Write a postcard to someone back home describing your voyage. Then, on the other side, draw a picture of something you saw on your trip.

Will the Real George Washington Carver Please Stand Up?

☆ Characters ☆

Host	Panelist 1
Biographer 1	Panelist 2
Biographer 2	Panelist 3
Carver 1	Panelist 4
Carver 2	Panelist 5
Carver 3	Panelist 6

Host: Welcome to *To Tell the Truth*! Today's guest is George Washington Carver, agriculturalist and educator. Of course, only one of our three guests is the real Dr. Carver. The other two are impostors. Listen carefully to what each one says. Then it's up to you to figure out who's telling the truth, the whole truth, and nothing but the truth. Let's begin by meeting our guests.

Carver 1: This may sound nuts to you, but my name is George Washington Carver.

Carver 2: Good day to you all. I'm George Washington Carver.

Carver 3: Greetings, everyone. My name is George Washington Carver.

Biographer 1: Before we start, the real Dr. Carver has asked us to read this letter of introduction to you:

> Dear Students: I, George Washington Carver, was born toward the end of the Civil War, in Diamond, Missouri. I can't tell you exactly when, because birth records weren't often kept about slave children like me. When I was a baby, bounty hunters kidnapped my mother and me from our owners, Moses and Susan Carver. I was soon found and returned to them, but I never saw my mother again.

Biographer 2: *(continues reading the letter)*

Growing up, I was fascinated by plant life. Eventually I went to college and then taught others the farming techniques that I learned. I discovered more than three hundred products that could be made from peanuts, and 118 uses for sweet potatoes. These alternative crops were crucial in the South, where farmers were ruining the soil with all the cotton they grew. I also had the idea of dehydrating foods and found a way to turn goldenrod sap into rubber. Not a bad career, huh? Signed, George Washington Carver

Host: Let's begin the questioning with Panelist 1.

Panelist 1: Though the Carvers were white, they raised you and your brother Jim almost like their own children. Jim would help in the fields while you, a more sickly child, learned how to cook, clean, and do laundry at home. You were also taught needlework and gardening. What would you say you were like as a child?

Carver 1: I was very shy. Given the choice, I would rather spend time alone in the woods or in my garden than with other people. There, I would collect toads, grasshoppers, feathers, and stones.

Carver 2: Because I was so sickly, I was always skinny. Some even said that my legs looked like matchsticks!

Carver 3: My voice was high-pitched, like the chirp of a frightened bird. That was probably because I damaged my vocal cords from coughing so much when I was young. Also, when I was excited, I sometimes stuttered.

Panelist 2: Neighbors nicknamed you "the plant doctor" because you were so good at treating sick plants. How did you learn so much about the natural world on your own?

Carver 1: I guess I always had a curious streak in me. I learned a lot simply by observing. Once I brought home some milkweed stalks so I could watch them open. Well, they opened alright . . . just as Mrs. Carver was cooking at the stove! Pod silk went everywhere! After that, I was told to do all of my observing outside!

Carver 2: Though I knew blizzards were dangerous, I was curious to know what it would be like to be out in one. So once, during a blizzard, I tied a rope around my bedpost. Then, holding tightly to the other end, I went outside. It was amazing. I couldn't see more than six inches in front of me, much less the house. But, clutching the rope, I was able to find my way home.

Carver 3: They say that necessity is the mother of invention. Maybe that's why I started using nature as a resource at such a young age. I once made a fiddle from a cornstalk and the hair of a horse's tail. Another time, I learned to knit by plucking two turkey feathers and unraveling an old mitten for wool. And once, after neighbors painted a mural on a wall of their house, I decided that I wanted to be a painter. So I found a way to make paints and a canvas from odds-and-ends around the house and in the woods.

Panelist 3: You appreciated that the Carvers taught you to read and write, but you wanted more of an education. Since the only school near their home did not admit black children, you left the Carvers at age twelve to attend a school that did. What happened to you next?

Carver 1: The nearest town that had a school for blacks was eight miles away, so that's where I went. There, I was lucky enough to be taken in by Mariah and Andrew Watkins, a childless black couple. Just as the Carvers had, they treated me like their own.

Carver 2: More than seventy pupils crammed into the one-room Lincoln School that I attended there. To pay for my school books, I helped Mrs. Watkins with the washing and ironing that she took in.

Carver 3: Before long, I had learned just about all I could at the Lincoln School. It was time to move on. And since I always had good grades, I was offered scholarships at a number of schools.

Panelist 4: In 1894, you graduated from Iowa State College in Ames, Iowa. Two years later, you earned a master's degree there. That year, the famous black educator, Booker T. Washington, came to see you. He offered you a job at his all-black school, Tuskegee Institute, in Alabama. You accepted. Why, with all of the job offers that you were receiving, did you decide on Tuskegee?

Carver 1: Mr. Washington offered me better benefits than any other school that contacted me. Besides, I thought it was nice that we both had "Washington" as part of our names!

Carver 2: I knew what it was like to be a poor black person trying to get an education, and I had always wanted to find a way to give back to my people. As a small black college in the South, Tuskegee offered me the chance to do just that.

Carver 3: I felt that Booker T. Washington and I had similar ideas about how to overcome prejudice. Both of us agreed that, rather than fight, it was better to work with whites, and show others that blacks were capable of learning and earning a respectable income.

Panelist 5: You must have loved Tuskegee, since you spent the rest of your life there. Besides finding uses for the peanut and the sweet potato, what else did you accomplish while living at the school?

Carver 1: Alabama was a perfect place for me to prove that there are uses for everything in nature. To me, a weed was simply a plant growing out of place. For example, I made rope from "useless" corn stalks. And I developed a type of plastic from wood shavings.

Carver 2: During World War II, Germany stopped supplying dyes to the United States. So I developed 536 new types of vegetable dyes from the leaves, stems, roots, and fruits of 28 different plants.

Carver 3: In addition to teaching in the classroom, I wrote many pamphlets on how to improve crop production. Then I traveled the Alabama countryside in an old painted wagon. Working from this "traveling school," I distributed the pamphlets to farmers and taught them other ways to improve their crops.

Panelist 6: As your fame grew, you were given nicknames like "the black DaVinci," "Columbus of the Soil," and "the Wizard of Tuskegee." But you also put up with a lot of bigotry. "Keep your thoughts free from hate," you once said, "and you need have no fear." What other words of wisdom were you known to give?

Carver 1: I once said, "A peanut a day keeps the doctor away." Or maybe that was "an apple a day . . . ." I really don't remember.

Carver 2: I truly believed that, "without genuine love of humanity, it is impossible to accomplish much."

Carver 3: I think I can proudly say that my life's work demonstrated my belief that "people must get the most out of nature before it is used up."

Host: Okay, everyone. It is now time to decide who you think is the real George Washington Carver. With a show of hands, how many think it is Carver 1? *(pause)* Carver 2? *(pause)* Carver 3? *(pause)* Now that everyone has voted, let's have the real George Washington Carver please stand up.

Will the Real George Washington Carver Please Stand Up?

☆ Teacher's Page ☆

Who Is the Real George Washington Carver?

Once all the votes have been cast, establish that Carver 2 is the real George Washington Carver. Then review the play, making sure that students can distinguish all of these true and false statements:

Panelists 1 and 2: All responses to the questions are true.

Panelist 3: Carver 3 is not telling the whole truth here. Carver worked hard, often taking in laundry, to put himself through college. Although Highland University in Kansas once offered him a scholarship, they withdrew the offer when they found out he was black. And, though he was finally admitted to Simpson College in Indianola, Iowa, he was denied student housing because of the color of his skin.

Panelist 4: This time, Carver 1 is not telling the truth. At that time, Tuskegee was still a fairly new—and very poor—college for black students. When Carver arrived, he wound up having to comb the school dump for bottles and jars simply to equip his lab!

Panelist 5: All responses to the questions are true.

Panelist 6: Both Carver 1 and Carver 3 are lying here. Carver 1's statement is simply a play on an old maxim, and the real George Washington Carver believed in working with nature, not using it up. He believed so strongly that "man is simply nature's agent or employee to assist her in her work," that he never took out any patents on his inventions. He felt that since God had given them to him, he had no right to claim them as his own.

Questions for Discussion

1. Why do you think George Washington Carver was called "the black DaVinci" and "Columbus of the soil"? Compare the accomplishments of Leonard DaVinci, Christopher Columbus, and Carver?

2. George Washington Carver didn't patent his ideas because he felt that they belonged to God, not to him. What is a patent? Do you agree with Carver? If you invented something, would you patent it? Why or why not?

3. What does the expression "necessity is the mother of invention" mean? How does it relate to George Washington Carver's life?

4. Carver once said, "To those who have as yet not learned the secret of true happiness, begin now to study the little things in your own door yard." What do you think he meant by that? Do you agree?

Activities

1. Rent the movie *The Autobiography of Jane Pitman* to see what life was like before the Civil War and up to the beginning of the Civil Rights Movement.

2. Have a "peanut celebration." Make homemade peanut butter, peanut soup, or peanut brittle. Be sure to check with parents before starting this activity in case any students in the class are allergic to peanuts.

3. Research some of the things that George Washington Carver was able to make from a peanut. Create a mural showing what they are.

Will the Real Helen Keller Please Stand Up?

☆ **Characters** ☆

Host	Panelist 1
Biographer 1	Panelist 2
Biographer 2	Panelist 3
Biographer 3	Panelist 4
Keller 1	Panelist 5
Keller 2	Panelist 6
Keller 3	

Host: Welcome to *To Tell the Truth*! Today's guest is Helen Keller, educator and spokesperson for the handicapped. Of course, only one of our three guests is the real Helen Keller. The other two are impostors. Listen carefully to what each one says. Then it's up to you to figure out who's telling the truth, the whole truth, and nothing but the truth. Let's begin by meeting our guests.

Keller 1: Hello, everyone. My name is Helen Keller.

Keller 2: Greetings to all of you. My name is Helen Keller.

Keller 3: Good day, students. My name is Helen Keller.

Biographer 1: Before we start, the real Helen Keller has asked us to read this letter of introduction to you:

Dear Students: I, Helen Keller, was born on June 27, 1880, in Tuscumbia, Alabama. At first, I was a healthy baby. But when I was nineteen months old, a "brain fever"—probably scarlet fever—left me deaf and blind. And, since I was not able to hear, I also became mute. I was like a music box with all the play shut up in me.

Biographer 2: *(continues reading the letter)*

Then, in March 1887, Anne Sullivan—a young teacher from the Perkins Institute in Boston, Massachusetts—came to live with our family. She had been sent to help me unlock my silent world. Anne was partially blind herself, so she appreciated my frustrations. This "miracle worker" helped me to understand what I could not see, and communicate with those who I could not hear. With her help, I became the first deaf and blind person to attend Radcliffe College, where I graduated with honors in 1899.

Biographer 3: *(continues reading the letter)*

For the rest of my life, I made it my goal to help others, especially the handicapped. And I gave talks around the world, hoping that my words would give the sighted and hearing a better understanding of disabled people like me. I also spoke out against racism and anti-Semitism, and supported many other causes. I died in 1968 at the age of eighty-eight. Signed, Helen Keller.

Host: Let's begin the questioning with Panelist 1.

Panelist 1:   After you lost your hearing and your sight, you became a frustrated, angry child. What can you tell us about your life before Anne Sullivan arrived?

Keller 1:   One time an aunt gave me a doll without a face to play with. So I pulled two beads off the cape that my aunt was wearing. Then I handed the doll and the beads to my mother. This was the only way I knew to explain that I wanted my new dollie to have eyes.

Keller 2:   When I once spilled water on my apron, I knew enough to lay the apron by the kitchen fire. But it didn't dry fast enough for me, so I moved it closer to the flames. Of course, I couldn't see what I was doing, and the apron caught fire. Incidents like this one made my parents wonder if it was safe for me to live at home.

Keller 3:   There was a cradle in our house that I would use with my dolls. But when my sister was born, my mother put her in there instead. That made me mad. One time I tipped the cradle over to get her out. Luckily, she wasn't hurt. But my parents grew even more concerned about the harm I could do.

Panelist 2:   It must have been frustrating for you, living in a dark and silent world, unable to communicate with anyone. In what ways would you try to make yourself heard?

Keller 1:   When I got really frustrated, I would break lamps, plates, or anything else I could get my hands on. And if I couldn't get someone's attention, I would pinch them quite hard!

Keller 2:   Sometimes I would touch people's faces. I could feel their throats vibrate and their lips move. I didn't understand that they were speaking, because I couldn't hear them. Yet, though their actions confused me, I'd try to imitate them.

Keller 3:   At an early age, I developed my own sign language. If I shivered, it meant I wanted ice cream. If I pulled my hair back, I wanted my mom. Putting imaginary eyeglasses on my face meant I wanted my father. In all, I had about sixty signs that I made up to help me communicate with the world.

Panelist 3:   The famous inventor Alexander Graham Bell, who also taught deaf students, suggested that your parents contact the Perkin's Institute for the Blind. The Institute sent Anne Sullivan to help you. What happened next?

Keller 1:   From the first day she arrived, Anne used a special manual alphabet to spell words into my hand. She was trying to show me that all objects have a name. At first, of course, I didn't understand what she was doing. I just thought that she was playing a game.

Keller 2:   One day we were out by a water pump, and she finger-spelled W-A-T-E-R into one hand as she placed my other hand under the spigot. Suddenly, something clicked, and I understood what she was doing. I learned thirty words that day, including my own name.

Keller 3:   About a month later Anne gave me my first spelling test, and I'm proud to say that I got an "A"!

Panelist 4:   Once you started learning, you didn't want to stop! You constantly pushed yourself to try things that sighted people could do. Can you give us a few examples of this, please?

Keller 1:   Sure. By tying a long rope around my waist, and then knotting the other end around a tree, I would sometimes go swimming all by myself!

Keller 2:   I enjoyed playing miniature golf with a special electronic chip which would beep enabling me to locate its position on the course.

Keller 3:   I had a specially made deck of cards and a checker set that I could use. I could also ride a bicycle built for two, as long as someone else steered!

Panelist 5:   As you got older, you decided that you wanted to go to college. Was it difficult to get into the school of your choice?

Keller 1: No. Many schools, including Cornell and the University of Chicago, wanted me. But I had made up my mind that I wanted to attend Radcliffe. It took me a while, though, to convince them that I could make the grade, despite my disabilities.

Keller 2: Given my disabilities, I knew it would be hard to get into any school. So I made up my mind to say okay to the first school that would take me. That school turned out to be Radcliffe.

Keller 3: Actually, Harvard would have been my first-choice school, but back in those days it was only open to men.

Panelist 6: After college, you supported many causes. Despite the fact that you couldn't hear, you learned to speak well enough to give lectures around the world. Besides working with groups like the American Foundation for the Blind, what other humanitarian work did you do?

Keller 1: During and after World War II, I visited soldiers who had been disabled in battle. By my own example, I tried to encourage them not to give up on life.

Keller 2: In 1959, the United Nations started the Helen Keller World Crusade. I was proud to know that, from then on, people would be working in my name to help deaf and blind children all over the globe.

Keller 3: Using a game that I invented called blindman's buff, I helped sighted schoolchildren learn to appreciate what it would be like to be blind.

Host: Okay, everyone. It is now time to decide who you think is the real Helen Keller. With a show of hands, how many think it is Keller 1? *(pause)* Keller 2? *(pause)* Keller 3? *(pause)* Now that everyone has voted, let's have the real Helen Keller please stand up.

Will the Real Helen Keller Please Stand Up?
☆ Teacher's Page ☆

Who Is the Real Helen Keller?

Once all the votes have been cast, establish that Keller 1 is the real Helen Keller. Then review the play, making sure that students can distinguish all of these true and false statements:

Panelists 1 and 2: All responses to the questions are true.

Panelist 3: Only Keller 3 is not telling the truth here. Anne Sullivan would not have been concerned after one month with how well Helen could spell!

Panelist 4: As surprising as it may be to some students, Keller 1 and 3 are telling the truth here. Only Keller 2 is lying. Helen could not have played miniature golf with a special ball with an electronic chip since this technology didn't exist at the time.

Panelist 5: Only Keller 2 is not telling the truth here. By the time Helen was ready to apply to college, many people had heard of her. Though some schools would have been happy to have her, others (including Radcliff) were concerned about how well she'd do in a traditional school setting where not all books were available in Braille. Helen, though, had her heart set on Radcliff. She was admitted there after passing their entrance exams.

Panelist 6: Only Keller 3 is not telling the truth here. The game blindman's buff has been around since as early as the 1600s.

Questions for Discussion

1. At first, Helen Keller's parents were critical of the way Anne Sullivan treated their child. They had always pampered Helen out of love, and they felt she couldn't know better when she did wrong. Do you think that those with disabilities should be treated any differently than other people? Why or why not?

2. If you had been Helen Keller's teacher, how might you have tried to help her make a connection between hand-spelling and words?

3. What do you think it would be like to lose your hearing, sight, speech, and/or mobility? Which disabilities do you think would be most difficult to deal with? What makes you think so?

4. Helen Keller once said that "self pity is our worst enemy and if we yield to it we can never do anything wise in the world." What do you think she meant by this? Do you agree? Why or why not?

Activities

1. Do some research about American Sign Language and Braille. Then try to communicate a sentence in each with a friend. (Note: To practice writing in Braille, use glue to raise up the dots.)

2. Wear a blindfold for ten minutes to help you imagine what it would be like to be blind. Then write a story about the experience.

3. After researching Louis Braille's life, write him a letter giving your opinions about the Braille alphabet.

Will the Real Dr. Martin Luther King, Jr. Please Stand Up?

☆ **Characters** ☆

Host	Panelist 1
Biographer 1	Panelist 2
Biographer 2	Panelist 3
Biographer 3	Panelist 4
King 1	Panelist 5
King 2	
King 3	

Host: Welcome to *To Tell the Truth*! Today's guest is Dr. Martin Luther King, Jr., the famous civil rights leader. Of course, only one of our three guests is the real Dr. King. The other two are impostors. Listen carefully to what each one says. Then it's up to you to figure out who's telling the truth, the whole truth, and nothing but the truth. Let's begin by meeting our guests.

King 1: Greetings, one and all! My name is Dr. Martin Luther King, Jr.

King 2: Hello, everybody. My name is Dr. Martin Luther King, Jr.

King 3: Thanks for inviting me here today. My name is Dr. Martin Luther King, Jr.

Biographer 1: Before we start, the real Dr. King has asked us to read this letter of introduction to you:

Dear Students: I, Martin Luther King, Jr., was born Michael Luther King in Atlanta, Georgia, in 1929. When I was six years old, both my father and I changed our names in honor of Martin Luther, founder of the Protestant faith. Later I studied to become a minister like my father and grandfather. In school, I learned about the teachings of Mahatma Gandhi, among others. This political leader had used nonviolence to fight injustice in India. I wondered if blacks could use similar methods to fight prejudice in the United States.

Biographer 2: *(continues reading the letter)*

Even with nonviolence, though, I knew that the struggle for civil rights would be dangerous. Many whites, especially in the South, had treated black people like second class citizens for a long time. But that didn't stop my followers and I. After many peace marches, protests, sit-ins, and boycotts, slowly but surely, we started to see changes being made.

Biographer 3: *(continues reading the letter)*

The biggest march I ever led took place in Washington D.C., in 1963. There, I gave a famous speech describing a world in which people "will not be judged by the color of their skin but by the content of their character." A year later, I became the youngest person to ever receive the Nobel Peace Prize. Eventually, though, hatred caught up with me. In 1968, I was assasinated by a racist named James Earl Ray. But my dream has not faded. Since 1986, my birthday has been a national holiday. Signed, Martin Luther King, Jr.

Host: Let's start the questioning with Panelist 1.

Panelist 1: You came from a family that valued education very highly. What kinds of things did you learn at a young age?

King 1: As soon as I was old enough, I started reading books about famous black Americans like Frederick Douglass, George Washington Carver, Jesse Owens, Booker T. Washington, and Harriet Tubman. All of them were heroes and role models to me.

King 2: My parents also inspired me. They taught me to stand proud, no matter what happens. One time, my dad and I were driving somewhere when a police officer pulled us over. "Show me your license, boy," he said disrespectfully to my father. But my dad looked him in the eye, then pointed to me. "He's a boy. I'm a man," he replied.

King 3: As a child, I did very well in the segregated school that I attended. I even skipped two grades. But on entering an integrated college, my test scores dropped. It turned out that the standards in my elementary school were not as high as they were in white public schools. I had to work hard to catch up. But, before long, my grades had improved.

Panelist 2: While you were growing up, many Southern states had "Jim Crow" laws on the books, limiting the rights of black people. There were signs everywhere telling African

Americans that they could only use certain restaurants, restrooms, and drinking fountains. Schools, movie theaters, parks, and playgrounds were also segregated. How else did you experience racism as a child?

King 1:   When I was very small, I was friends with the son of the local grocery store owner. Then we both started school. He went to a whites-only school, and I went to a school for black children. From then on, his parents wouldn't let us play together. They felt that, as we got older, we should start playing with "our own kind."

King 2:   Once, my father and I went into a shoestore and sat down. But the storekeeper said he wouldn't help us unless we moved to the "colored" section in the back. "We'll either buy shoes sitting here or we won't buy shoes at all," my father said. Then we walked out.

King 3:   When I was fourteen, I won second place in a contest for a speech I wrote called, "The Negro and the Constitution." I remember that the bus ride back home from the ceremony was crowded. Eventually, the driver ordered me to stand up so that a white person could sit down. I obeyed—but it made me very angry!

Panelist 3:   You say that you were influenced by Mahatma Gandhi's philosophy of nonviolence. Were there other famous thinkers who also made an impression on you?

King 1:   About a hundred years before I was born, a New England philosopher named Henry David Thoreau wrote, "If a law is unjust, men should refuse to cooperate with it. They should even be willing to go to jail for not obeying such a law." Thoreau called this "civil disobedience." I liked that idea.

King 2:   Martin Luther, the sixteenth-century religious leader I was named after, once said. "To go against your conscience—your sense of right and wrong—is neither safe nor right." I agreed with that, too.

King 3:   As an adult I reread the works of one of my childhood heroes, Frederick Douglass. He wrote, "If there is no struggle, there is no progress." That idea also made sense to me.

Panelist 4:   As an adult, you worked hard trying to desegregate the South. What things did you do to bring about change?

King 1:   On December 1, 1955, a Montgomery, Alabama, black woman named Rosa Parks refused to give up her seat on a bus to a white person. She was actually arrested for that! Along with other city leaders, I helped put together a boycott. As a pastor, I asked my congregation to stop taking buses until the law was changed. Our boycott lasted about a year, but finally we won. In November 1956, the Supreme Court ruled that the bus segregation law had to go.

King 2:   In the early 1960s, Birmingham, Alabama, was perhaps the most segregated city in the country. On April 12, 1963, I started leading marches through the streets there. The press covered the marches, and people all around the United States saw how badly Birmingham blacks were being treated. Even children were arrested! We received so much public support, that the unjust laws were finally changed.

King 3:   In August of 1965, in a black neighborhood of Los Angeles called "Watts," a riot began when a white police officer used unnecessary violence to arrest a black man. I was so mad, I couldn't take it anymore. I went to Watts and joined the others. By the time the Watts riots ended, thirty-four people were dead.

Panelist 5:   During your life, you gave many famous public speeches. What are some of your most famous words of wisdom that people will remember you by?

King 1:   I once said, "A penny saved is a penny earned."

King 2:   In 1964, I flew to Oslo, Norway, to accept the Nobel Peace Prize. But when I returned, I knew it was time to get back to work. While addressing an audience in Atlanta, Georgia, I said, "These past few weeks I have been on a mountaintop. And I really wish I could just stay on that mountain. But I must go back to the valley. I must go back because there are people who can't vote in the valley, and people who are starving, and people who don't have jobs." From there, I headed to Selma, Alabama.

King 3:   After leading a fifty-mile march from Selma to Montgomery, Alabama, in 1965, I stood on the steps of the state capitol and led the people in a chorus of "Sweet Home Alabama."

Host: Okay, everyone. It is now time to decide who you think is the real Martin Luther King, Jr. With a show of hands, how many think it is King 1? *(pause)* King 2? *(pause)* King 3? *(pause)* Now that everyone has voted, let's have the real Martin Luther King, Jr., please stand up.

Will the Real Martin Luther King, Jr. Please Stand Up?
✫ Teacher's Page ✫

Who Is the Real Martin Luther King, Jr.?

Once all the votes have been cast, establish that King 2 is the real Martin Luther King, Jr. Then review the play, making sure that students can distinguish all of these true and false statements:

Panelists 1, 2, and 3: All responses to the questions are true.

Panelist 4: The Watts riots did take place in 1965, as described. However, when Dr. King arrived, he tried to stop the riots peacefully; he did not take part in them. Thus, King 3 is not telling the whole truth here.

Panelist 5: King 1 and 3 are lying. Benjamin Franklin is known for saying, "A penny saved is a penny earned," and King would not have sung a song praising Alabama. When King reached the steps of the capitol in Montgomery, Alabama, he said, "They told us we wouldn't get here. And there were those who said that we would get here only over their dead bodies. But all the world today knows that we are here, and standing before the forces of power in the State of Alabama saying 'We ain't goin' let nobody turn us around.' So I stand before you today with the conviction that segregation is on its death bed." Then he led the people in a chorus of "We Have Overcome."

Questions for Discussion

1. Compare what it was like growing up African American when Dr. King was a boy with what it's like to be black today. How are things better? Are any things the same, or worse? If so, what?

2. In what ways do you think Martin Luther King, Jr.'s, experiences as a child affected the work that he decided to do in his later life?

3. Mahatma Gandhi, Henry David Thoreau, and Martin Luther King, Jr., all believed in civil disobedience. Do you? What should you do if there are laws with which you don't agree? If you were Rosa Parks, would you have obeyed the law and given up your bus seat for a white person? Why or why not?

Activities

1. Dr. King's famous "I Have a Dream" speech is available from many sources. After reading or listening to a copy of it, discuss how Dr. King was able to inspire people. Then write your own speech, trying to convince others of something that you believe.

2. Research additional information about the beliefs of Henry David Thoreau, Mahatma Gandhi, and Martin Luther. Create a chart showing how their beliefs were similar, and how they differed.

3. As a class, identify a local situation that everyone agrees is unfair. Put together a plan of action to change it.

✳ Additional Resources ✳

Christopher Columbus

✳ *Christopher Columbus* by David Goodnough (Troll Associates, 1979).

✳ *Christopher Columbus* by Nancy Levinson (Lodestar Books, 1990).

✳ Christopher Columbus: Extracts From Journal
http://www.fordham.edu/halsall/source/columbus1.html

✳ Columbus Day
http://deil.lang.uiuc.edu/web.pages/holidays/Columbus.html

✳ *Where Do You Think You're Going, Christopher Columbus?* by Jean Fritz (Putnam, 1980).

Benjamin Franklin

✳ *Benjamin Franklin* by Charles P. Graves (Garrard Publishing Company, 1960).

✳ *Benjamin Franklin* (Heroes of the Revolution series) by Susan and John Lee (Children's Press, 1974).

✳ Benjamin Franklin: Glimpses of the Man
http://sln.fi.edu/franklin/

✳ *Benjamin Franklin: The New American* by Milton Meltzer (Franklin Watts, 1988).

✳ Quotations: Life in Franklin's Own Words
http:library.thinkquest.org/22254/frquot.htm

✳ *What's the Big Idea, Benjamin Franklin?* by Jean Fritz (Coward, McCann and Geoghegan,1976).

Daniel Boone

✳ *Daniel Boone, Westward With American Explorers* by Walter Buehr (G.P. Putnam, 1963).

✳ *Daniel Boone, Wilderness Pioneer* by Carl R. Green and William R. Sanford (Enslow Publishers, 1997).

✳ *Famous Pioneers* by Franklin Folsom (Harvey House, 1964).

✳ *Fighting Frontiersman: The Life of Daniel Boone* by John Bakeless (William and Morrow, 1948).

✳ *Frontier Leaders and Pioneers* by Dorothy Heiderstadt (David McKay Publishing, 1962).

✳ The Lives of Famous Americans:Daniel Boone
http://earlyamerica.com/lives/boone/index.html

✳ *Men of the Wild Frontier* by Bennett Wayne (Garrard Publishers, 1974).

Paul Revere

✳ *A Picture Book of Paul Revere* by David A. Adler (Holiday House, 1995).

✳ *And Then What Happened, Paul Revere?* by Jean Fritz (Coward, McCann and Geoghegan, Inc. 1973).

✳ Paul Revere House
http://www.paulreverehouse.org/

✳ *Paul Revere: The Man Behind the Legend* by Margaret Green (Julian Messner, 1964).

Dolley Madison

✳ *Dolley Madison* by Patricia Ryon Quiri (Franklin Watts Press, 1993).

✳ Dolley Madison on the Burning of Washington
http://www.nationalcenter.org/WashingtonBurning1814.html

✳ *Dolley Payne Todd Madison* by Alice K. Flanagin (Children's Press, 1997).

✳ White House for Kids
http://www.whitehouse.gov/kids/index.html

Sacagawea

✳ *American Indian Women* by Marion E. Gridley (Hawthorn Books, 1974).

✳ *Famous Women of America* by William Oliver Stevens (Dodd, Mead and Company, 1950).

✳ Lewis and Clark: Living History
http://www.pbs.org/lewisandclark/living/idx_4.html

✳ New Perspectives on the West
http://www.pbs.org/weta/thewest/wpages/wpgs400/w4sacaga.htm

✳ *Sacagawea* by Betty Westrom Skold (Dillion Press, 1977).

✳ *Sacagawea* by Olive Burt (Franklin Watts, 1978).

✳ *Sacagawea, Bird Girl* by Fiora Warren Seymour (Bobbs Merrill, 1959).

Abraham Lincoln

✳ *Abraham Lincoln* by Ingri and Edgar Parin d'Aulaire (Doubleday, 1957).

✳ *Abraham Lincoln* by Susan Dye Lee (Childrens Press, 1978).

✳ *Abraham Lincoln, A First Book* by Larry Metzzer (Franklin Watts, 1987).

✳ Abraham Lincoln: An Educational Site
http://www.geocities.com/SunsetStrip/Venue/5217/lincoln.html

✳ *Abraham Lincoln, Friend of the People* by Clara Ingram Judson (Wilcox and Follett, 1950).

✳ Abraham Lincoln Online
http://www.netins.net/showcase/creative/lincoln.html

✳ *America's Abraham Lincoln* by May McNeer (Houghton Mifflin, 1957).

✳ *The Great American Series: Abraham Lincoln* by Kathie Billingslea Smith (Julian Messner, 1987).